MURDER ON THE MAIL

Rumbles on the Rails Book Two

MICHAEL CLUTTERBUCK

HEDDON PUBLISHING

First edition published in 2024 by Heddon Publishing.

Copyright © Michael Clutterbuck 2024, all rights reserved. No part of this book may be reproduced, adapted, stored in a retrieval system or transmitted by any means, electronic, photocopying, or otherwise without prior permission of the author.

Print ISBN 978-1-913166-92-2
Ebook ISBN 978-1-913166-93-9

Cover design by Catherine Clarke Design
www.catherineclarkedesign.co.uk

This is a work of fiction. Names, characters, businesses, places, events and incidents are either the products of the author's imagination or used in a fictitious manner. Any resemblance to actual persons, living or dead, or actual events is purely coincidental.

www.heddonpublishing.com
www.facebook.com/heddonpublishing
@PublishHeddon

Michael Clutterbuck is a retired schoolteacher living in Melbourne, Australia with his wife, two children and five grandchildren. He was born in 1937, brought up in Chester in a railway family, and was educated at the King's School and Manchester University. After his training as a language teacher, he spent four years in Hamburg, where he married. He and his wife migrated to Australia in 1965. He spent twenty-five years teaching at a school in Melbourne, followed by another twelve years teaching academic English to young Asian adults at Monash University, finally retiring in 2004. He co-authored a set of English exam preparation tests before writing the *Steaming Into* series of seven books of railway fiction published by Heddon in the UK. *Murder on the Mail* is the second book in a new series of railway crime stories.

Praise for the Steaming Into series

"One of the best books of its kind. Hats off to the author. So good I have bought all the other books in the same series."

"Right from the start you could smell the smoke and hear the clank of metal wheels on iron rails. Back to a time of the dark days of war. The men who worked so hard to keep the country moving the story runs from the beginning of the war though to the end. A story that in parts is funny and in others so sad, I found this a good read for the start of what life was like for the men who ran it, a time now long gone but still remembered."

"Being a steam enthusiast I am probably biased, but this book is an extremely good history of what it was like to be operating steam trains during the bombing. This author has apparently written more books on the subject which I intend to read. Very absorbing."

"When I first read this, I couldn't believe it was a work of fiction. The author has done his research into the intricacies and politics of men working on the steam locomotive footplate. The attention to detail is brilliant the background stories are also very interesting. Highly recommended to those who have an interest in Steam Locomotives and the crews that worked on them."

This is for Christa

INTRODUCTION

As a youngster I once saw the film *Train of Events*, made in 1949 and still well worth having a look at. The railway scenes immediately after the nationalisation of the railways are so authentic – unlike some of the text. Jack Warner as Driver Hardcastle remarks to a colleague that he is taking the express with an engine "of the Royal Scot class". He would be far more likely to say something like, "I'm on the Liverpool sleeper with a rebuilt Scot," or "on the down Liverpool with a new Scot." But I suppose that might confuse an audience unfamiliar with railway parlance. I watched it again recently and thought, *Now there's an idea; I wonder if I could write something along those lines myself: a number of diverse stories rolled into one train journey.* So I had a go.

Kath, my long-term advisor/editor, liked it and put her editorial stamp on it, waving her wizard wand and revising my rantings, which in my view greatly improves the story, although that of course is for readers to judge. Readers wishing to know more of the friendship between Driver O'Leary and Fireman Winslowe are recommended to consult *Steaming into the North West* (also published by Heddon).

Readers might be interested to learn that the name of the train, the 'Irish Mail' is thought to be the longest-lasting name of any train in Britain, lasting over 150 years, from 1848 to 2002.

Michael Clutterbuck, Melbourne. 2024.

Railway Map

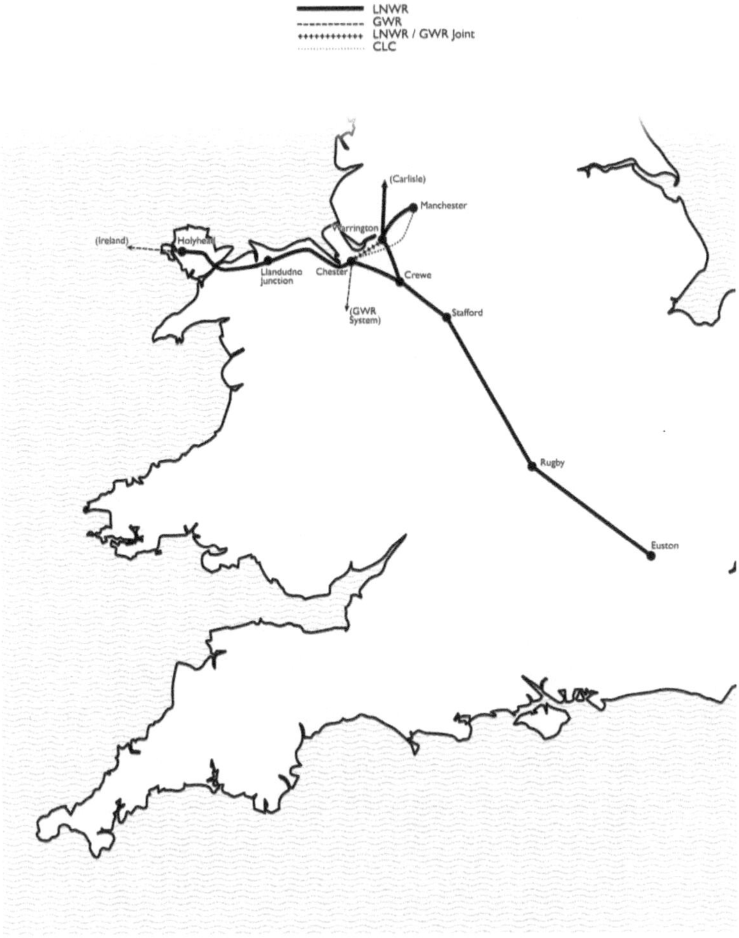

LNWR
GWR
LNWR / GWR Joint
CLC
(Carlisle)
Manchester
Warrington
(Ireland)
Holyhead
Llandudno Junction
Chester
Crewe
(GWR System)
Stafford
Rugby
Euston

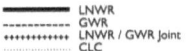

Prologue

The mighty London and North Western Railway was keen to emphasise its success, calling itself 'The Premier Line'. It was by some measure the largest railway company in the United Kingdom. In fact, the L&NWR claimed to be the world's largest private company. Naturally, this could depend on how you manipulated statistics, but it was certainly the largest in the United Kingdom.

The L&NWR built their own locomotives and even made their own steel from which to manufacture them. They claimed to be "The quickest and most comfortable route between London and Birmingham, Manchester, Liverpool, Ireland, Scotland, etc, etc." Now, while this might have been true for much of the time, it emphatically could not have applied to the journey on the evening 'Irish Mail' between Euston and Holyhead one autumn day in 1913.

There were several distinct threads to the events which occurred in connection with this remarkable train journey, and several key players:

Mr Jonathon Gregory: an ambitious businessman keen to acquire a collection of jewels.
Mr Henry Smeddle: a knowledgeable jeweller with dubious ethics.

Mr Gordon Lowe: attempting to escape from a fuming and vengeful aristocrat after having seriously led astray the aforesaid noble's daughter.

Mr Jeffrey Waterman: an occasional employee of the angry aristocrat, tasked with arranging the required vengeance on Mr Lowe.

Len 'Thumper' Dawson: accompanying Mr Waterman and endowed with an impressive build and a fondness for inflicting violence.

James Dixon and Harriet Thornton-Legge: a pair of young lovers planning to travel to Scotland before their parents could interfere with their intention to marry.

Mr Colin Hampton: a private detective, in hot pursuit – if such a lethargic person could be described as hot anything – of the young, as yet unmarried, couple with a view to frustrating their romantic intentions.

Lady Denise Marchant: abandoning London Society after having seriously embarrassed herself during a ball at Count Montague Fitchworth's City residence.

Canon Glyn Jones of Deganwy: his leave in London had been interrupted and was travelling to Holyhead to meet his bishop, nervous about the latter's suspicions relating to the worthy canon's private inclinations.

An additional thread were three employees of the LNWR itself, namely the enginemen in the cab as well as the train guard.

In the cab of the locomotive: Driver Patrick O'Leary

and Fireman Johnny Winslowe, who had found themselves in charge of one of the London and North Western Railway's brand new express engines for the first time.

In the train's brake van was Guard Herbert Simmons.

Last and by no means least are Mr Edward Thorpe and Detective Chief Inspector Vincent Brown.

Thorpe was employed by Sir Alexander Wetherby to guard his luggage, travelling in the guard's van along with Herbert Simmons.

Meanwhile, in his office in London, DCI Brown was quietly pulling strings.

CHAPTER 1

The first Threads

The old warehouse stood at the corner of a road in an impoverished area of Limehouse, near the docks of the Thames. It had stood empty for some years now and the word was that it was to be demolished, but the owners were clearly in no particular hurry. A man in heavily-used work clothing, possibly a dockyard worker, strolled around the corner and stood waiting and watching. A moment or two later two young women, one holding onto a small child, appeared out of a side street, gossiping.

Daisy Walker was a tall, lanky woman with a lined face although she could not have passed the age of twenty-five. Her little son was no more than five years old. Daisy's friend Emma Sinclair was much younger than her, perhaps eighteen, and was carrying a basket with a loaf of bread and some vegetables. Both ladies were rather shabbily dressed, as were nearly all women in this working-class district of London, where fashionably attired people were liable to attract unwelcome attention.

The ladies stopped as one and stared in disbelief as

an elegant gentleman in a grey top hat walked round the corner, stopped at the warehouse door, and looked over the road.

"Cor! Yer see the toff, Em?" gasped Daisy.

"Ay, Daze, I did. Wot's a gent like that doin' dahn 'ere?"

The workman walked over the road towards them.

"Yer didn't see nuffin!" he growled.

"An' 'oo are you, ter tell us wot we saw?" Daisy demanded truculently.

The man grabbed the little boy, pulled a knife out of his jacket, and snarled, "I'm a cove wiv a shiv. Yer didn't see nuffin'. Now piss orf quick!"

Daisy, deciding with some regret that this was neither the time nor place for a vigorous and entertaining argument, seized her child from the man and hurried away with Emma. As they left, the gentleman tossed a shilling across the road to the workman with a nod of thanks and entered the warehouse.

In the gloomy, echoing space, the gentleman joined a middle-aged man who was sitting at a rickety table. There were two large candles on the table, with a map of England and Wales spread out on it. The two men began a discussion, pointing to various places on the map.

The older of the two, a man named Henry Smeddle, appeared to be of lesser taste, yet his clothing belied his profession as a jeweller. He was dressed in a threadbare and collarless jacket and heavily worn trousers with string tied round them just below the knees. His grubby face had seen neither water nor a razor that day.

Smeddle's suave companion, known to all but his wife as Jonathon Gregory (to his wife he was Jonathon Clayton) glared at him.

"What in heaven's name are you dressed like that for, Smeddle?" he queried in distaste. "You look like a common workman!" Gregory himself was dressed in a clean dark jacket, smart striped trousers, and polished boots. His top hat sat on the table next to the map.

"I am very well aware of my curious appearance, Mr Gregory," replied Smeddle, "but I believe that in this district and dressed as I am, I would be highly unlikely to draw attention to myself, whereas—" He stopped himself just in time, realising that what he was about to say could be taken as a criticism of Gregory. This would not only be impolite, it would be foolhardy. Gregory was known to have a short temper and, more to the point, to also have a number of associates who were not above supplying violent retribution if requested.

"Whereas…?" Gregory's expression was questioning, causing Smeddle to rapidly reconsider his reply. "Whereas, I was going to say, had I dressed in my normal attire, Mr Gregory, then my business suit and the rings on my fingers might have been rather tempting for any local undesirables."

"I see."

Smeddle was unsure whether the rapid change in what he had been about to say had mollified

Gregory, and decided to say nothing more that could get him deeper down the mire into which he might already have dug himself.

Gregory was interested in Smeddle. Not only was he an upmarket jeweller, he also seemed to be knowledgeable about the seamier side of the trade. What Gregory did not know was that Smeddle had easy access to another jeweller, Frederick Harwood. Mr Harwood had an unobtrusive little establishment in an equally unobtrusive side alley and took great care to show no interest whatsoever in the source of items offered to him for sale. This enabled him to offer low prices for a speedy transaction, suiting many of his customers, who were sometimes keen for a conveniently rapid disposal of the items they had acquired (often in the small hours of the previous night). Harwood kept really valuable items in a hidden safe for at least six months before selling them on at a tidy profit, which explained why he had not yet been called into the local constabulary to explain details of his purchases.

But Smeddle himself had been the subject of detailed scrutiny. Gregory had formed a plan requiring the knowledge of a competent jeweller with malleable ethics. He had approached a senior police detective on the force with a request for a recommendation of an honest and reliable jeweller to value his large (as yet fictitious) jewellery collection. On hearing mention of Smeddle's name, Detective Chief Inspector Vincent Brown had shaken his head.

"In all honesty, Mr Gregory, I could not recommend Mr Smeddle. Having said that, however, the police have nothing officially against his name. I can say nothing more on the matter."

Gregory nodded sagely whilst inwardly celebrating; Smeddle sounded exactly the sort of man he needed. As if that wasn't enough, his visit to the DCI had an unexpected bonus. As Gregory was leaving, he overheard Brown demanding to see a Sergeant Thorpe, to explain a serious breach of police procedure which could very likely lead to the sergeant's dismissal. Might a later quiet word to this sergeant lead to a profitable financial arrangement? Gregory made a mental note of the sergeant's name. A contact with insider knowledge of the police force could offer definite advantages, as could an ex-policeman with expert knowledge and a grudge against the force.

***

One of Gregory's aristocratic acquaintances, Sir Alexander Wetherby, owned a large estate in Ireland and Sir Alexander had decided to live there for a few years with his wife and family. He had a certain sympathy with the view that Ireland should be ruled from Dublin rather than from Westminster, and if that did not suit his noble friends in the House of Lords, so be it. He had further determined to take quite a substantial amount of his property with him. This included his extensive jewellery collection, which Sir Alexander had once proudly shown to Gregory. The latter had little interest in politics; his own interest was far more closely aligned with the increase in his personal wealth. His politics, should they ever assist in this endeavour, would need to be modified accordingly.

Sir Wetherby's jewellery display had included six or seven items which Gregory had privately concluded ought to form the basis of his own future collection. He had carefully noted the details of the items of interest but needed the advice of a competent jeweller about finding paste copies, or perhaps similar but cheap replacements, should the opportunity for a surreptitious exchange arise. He would also like to hear of methods of safeguarding the transport of such a collection, and thus better prepare to frustrate such safeguards. Judging by what DCI Brown had said, Smeddle appeared to be the ideal man.

Gregory realised he would also need the advice of a railway or postal official; someone who was either gullible or who could be bribed, would suffice.

He would discover which pub Sergeant Thorpe drank in; he looked to be a potential assistant. Jonathon Gregory was already a man of some means, but he wished to become what Americans were beginning to call a millionaire.

***

A horse-drawn cab hurried along Gower Street and swerved into Euston Road before swinging again under the great arch and onto the concourse at Euston Railway Station. The passenger jumped out with a quick handover of a ten-shilling note to the grinning cabby and raced into the station booking hall. He booked a ticket to Holyhead and walked rapidly onto the departure platform where the evening Irish Mail train was ready to depart fifteen minutes later.

The huge locomotive was hissing gently in its gleaming blackberry-black with grey, red, and cream lining, which gave it a very smart appearance indeed; this was only enhanced by the coaches themselves, in their plum lower halves and white upper sections with yellow edging.

The passenger with a small Gladstone bag hurried along the platform, glancing nervously behind as he searched for a compartment in a third-class carriage. Finding one, he shot a quick look around as he entered and shut the door. He shuffled carefully past the other seated passengers and, ignoring two vacant seats, reached the corridor and left the compartment. He eased his way along to a third-class compartment in another coach before entering and taking a seat there.

There was good reason for this excessive caution.

Some five months previously, Gordon Lowe had seen the young Hon. Rosemarie Morton with a group of her friends in a restaurant in Regent Street, and taken a strong fancy to her. She was clearly, he observed, the leading female in her group as the other young ladies – older schoolgirls, he assumed from their uniform dress – were seemingly there at her invitation. Lowe watched the group during their Kaffeklatsch, as they called it, until they broke up to leave. He heard them refer to his target as Rosy as they said their goodbyes and left.

Rosy opened her bag to put a purse on the table while she carefully adjusted her hat, glancing into a nearby mirror on the wall. Lowe stood up, leaving his own hat on his seat, and sidled past her, unobtrusively transferring her purse from the table to his pocket. Although he was not a regular pickpocket, he liked to keep his hand in from time to time. You never knew when such skill might be useful.

"Is there a problem, miss?" The waitress saw Rosy searching for something and came over to assist; sympathetic help was often a sure way of increasing a tip.

"Oh, yes indeed. I have mislaid my purse. I'm sure I placed it on the table a moment ago; it must have slipped off onto the floor, yet I cannot find it."

The waitress was privately disappointed; it was normally elderly ladies who tried this on. There would be no tip here, just a tiresome discussion with the head waiter. She was about to call him over, but a gentleman came over to pass them.

Excusing himself, he said, "I think I left my hat on my seat." Then, appearing to see the young lady had a problem, he directed an enquiry to Rosy herself, ignoring the waitress. "Is there some difficulty I can help with, miss?"

"Yes," replied Rosy. "I seem to have mislaid my purse. I am certain I placed it on the table while I secured my hat in place. It must have fallen onto the floor but for the life of me I cannot find it."

The gentleman retrieved his hat and bowed to the young lady. "My name is Lowe, miss. Gordon Lowe. Please allow me to settle your account." He turned to the waitress, "How much is this young lady's bill?"

"It's seven shillings, sir."

The man selected a half-sovereign from his pocket. "That should see the matter closed, I think," he said to the waitress, who bobbed a delighted curtsey. Cor blimey, a whole three bob tip!

"Allow me to escort you out of this restaurant," Gordon Lowe said to Rosy, offering her his arm. She accepted with a nod of thanks, as if it were her due. After they left, the waitress bent down to search for the missing purse. If she could find it, she might even get another shilling or two as a reward.

"You must be rather put out by the unfortunate episode." Lowe spoke solicitously in the street outside. "Perhaps you would like to sit down in the park across the road and spend a few moments recovering yourself?"

"Thank you, sir, I should appreciate that." Mama's warning about talking to strange men popped into Rosy's mind but she pushed it away. Mama had not met such a nice man. However, as they walked across the road the clouds, already threatening, opened up, and heavy rain began to fall.

"Oh dear," said Lowe, looking at the sky. "This does not appear to be a shower. Look, miss, my house is nearby. Would you like to shelter there until the weather is rather more friendly? My butler will assist you with a refreshing beverage, I'm sure."

"That is really most kind of you, sir, but I do not wish to put you to any trouble." Rosy thought again of the warning but dismissed it: the man had a butler and if he could afford a butler he had to be a gentleman. *With all due respect to Mama*, thought Rosy, *she really lives in the last century.*

"Not at all, miss. You are very welcome." Lowe held Rosy's arm and guided her along the road. After ten minutes they arrived at his residence. Looking around, Rosy was impressed. Very acceptable, she thought. She might even give him a kiss when she finally left.

Once in the house, Lowe settled Rosy into a comfortable sofa and rang for his butler. Nobody appeared.

"Oh goodness! How remiss of me!" muttered Lowe in annoyance. "It is Jenkin's day off. I had completely forgotten! Just wait here miss, and I'll fetch you a drink myself." He returned two minutes later with a large brandy and a towel. "Here, miss, this will ease your discomfort. It has a thimble-full of brandy topped up with a large amount of water, as I do not believe you are much over sixteen. Then I shall show you to the bathroom, where you can remove your coat and freshen up a little."

Hearing this, Rosy felt a tingle of excitement; the girls at school often fantasised about such a situation. Might it happen to her? And if it did, would she enjoy it?

"That is really very kind of you, sir. I am most appreciative."

But although Rosy had been brought up in good society, she had not been exposed to strong alcohol. The large drink, containing rather more brandy that Lowe had implied (and another ingredient which Lowe had omitted to mention), relaxed her to the extent that she did not resist Lowe when he took her to the bathroom, removed her coat, then proceeded to remove further garments.

Two hours later she was put, still semi-comatose and a little sore, into a coach and driven home, where her mother took one look at her and immediately sent her to bed and had a doctor summoned. His consultation was brief but alarming.

"I very much regret to say, my lady, that your daughter is inebriated and likely under the influence of some drug, although I cannot be sure about that. She will have an aching head tomorrow but should suffer no further harm on that score. I fear, however, that she has also been the victim of, um undue physical attention and that it is quite possible the consequences may be clearly visible in a matter of months."

When Lord Edale was informed of his daughter's possible condition, he immediately paled with worry but then reversed his facial hue into a bright puce as fury took over.

"I want that man found and horsewhipped!" he raged. "Herriott!" he called over his shoulder, and the butler hurried forward. "Yes, m'lud?"

"Telephone instantly for the police. I want a senior detective here within the hour."

"At once, m'lud." Herriott retreated to carry out his lordship's command.

By one of those curious coincidences, Detective Chief Inspector Brown arrived. He was not, however, as helpful as his lordship had expected.

"I need a description of the alleged perpetrator, my lord," he explained.

"My daughter is in bed and cannot be disturbed, Mr Brown."

"Then the address of the residence where the attack is alleged to have taken place?"

"No idea, man. That is your job to discover."

"Perhaps the cafeteria, where your daughter met the man?"

"Don't you listen, fellow? I said my daughter cannot be disturbed!"

"With all due respect, my lord, police investigators work with clues. The total absence of these hampers us somewhat. I will return to speak with your daughter as soon as she is able to answer questions. Good evening, Lord Edale." DCI Brown turned on his heel and marched out.

"That man is useless!" raved his lordship. "He has no respect for his betters. Herriott, call that thug Waterman and tell him to get another man, find that rascal, and teach him not to interfere with my daughter. When I hear the man is seriously injured in hospital, there will be a hundred pounds for them."

"Certainly, m'lud."

Thus it was that while Lowe had been unaware that Rosy was the daughter of a lord, he had read the local paper in which a report of the 'suspected impertinence to Lord Edale's daughter' had appeared. His lordship was said to have called up a local private detective to look into the affair, claiming a failing on the part of the local police. Lowe knew, as did many in the neighbourhood, of Lord Edale's public irascibility and determination once he had decided upon an action. Lowe had concluded that a speedy visit to a far location was desirable. The actual destination was of lesser importance than its distance.

Yet despite his caution, Lowe did not catch sight of the two men following him. Thumper Dawson was a large man with a liking for using his fists. His smaller partner, Jeff Waterman, provided what thinking was required to carry out their assignments. Waterman enjoyed working with his large friend but knew that care was needed: Thumper was emphatically not the sharpest knife in the drawer. He was more your 'thump and scarper' artist; but while the thumping was fine, the scarpering on a train had limits, and needed Waterman's brain.

***

Months earlier, over the warehouse table, Gregory had explained his basic idea to Smeddle. "My target plans to travel next month to Ireland, Smeddle. He will book a first-class seat on the Irish Mail travelling with the London and North Western Railway from Euston to Holyhead." He traced the route on the map with his finger. "His belongings, including his jewellery, will go carefully locked in the luggage van under the eye of a private guard. This is the man we must somehow distract while you check the jewellery case. I need you to find and bring replacement items for the half-dozen jewels I have described to you, so that the theft will not be immediately obvious."

Smeddle nodded. "I'm sure I can be of use." That didn't sound too difficult; he had been given Gregory's sketches and he would contact Harwood to see whether he had any suitable replacements.

At home that evening, Gregory was discussing his plans with his wife. Edna was ten years younger than her husband and was attractive as well as ambitious and intelligent. Gregory had chosen her for these very qualities. She appeared to be able to hold her own in good society and to handle eager, lustful young men with practised ease. Her abilities were even more impressive with elderly, lecherous husbands. Indeed, Gregory would have been very surprised had he known quite how extensive her dealings with men had already been. Her six months' experience on the streets of Piccadilly had been quite something of a trial, but nevertheless they were very profitable and had taught her well. She had only exchanged her place of employment for high society to find a suitable – that is to say wealthy – husband.

In society, Gregory had exploited her abilities on one or two occasions to relieve rich husbands of items of value. His method had been to leave her alone with bored, married gentlemen, whose carnal desires Edna had seemingly encouraged in admiring an item of jewellery the victim had been showing off. But after receiving it as a gift, the delectable Edna had apparently completely misunderstood its purpose, and had objected vigorously and loudly to her companion's attempted intimate reward. Her outraged husband would storm into the room and threaten the unfortunate victim with the law, thus destroying his chances of a place in society. An instant apology would be proffered, and reluctantly accepted, and the incident closed with Mr and Mrs Clayton in possession of a valuable addition to their jewellery collection.

However, Gregory knew very well that this ploy had a limited life and could one day backfire and produce unwelcome consequences to himself. He needed another means of extending his collection. He had been uncertain as to how to do this until he met Sir Alexander Wetherby, and learned of the latter's move to Ireland by train. He recalled with private admiration the details fifty years back of a train robbery of gold from the Crimea military pay, organised by Tester, Pierce and Agar. He thought there would be something similar that he might be able to arrange, the only notable variation being that he would not be caught. He recognised that of enormous benefit would be the willing co-operation of a senior official and a competent jeweller.

A trip on the Irish Mail to Holyhead also seemed to be indicated, to survey the scene of activity. It was, of course, possible that the jewellery exchange might be easier on the ferry journey; well, he would travel and see how the land lay, so to speak.

After his visit to DCI Brown, he had discovered that Sergeant Thorpe, whose name he had heard as he left the DCI, had indeed been dismissed from the police force and Gregory had traced him to his regular pub. He slipped into the Crown and Anchor one evening as he saw Thorpe entering and went to the bar, standing next to the man. Thorpe had just received his pint when Gregory knocked his arm, tipping over some of Thorpe's beer.

"Oh damn! I am so sorry. Here, let me buy you another pint." Gregory's apology was effusive.

"Thanks, you can," Thorpe replied, surprised. "Good of you."

"Not at all, it was my fault entirely."

And over their drinks, the two men got chatting.

"Haven't seen you here before," said Thorpe. "You new around here?"

"Sort of," responded Gregory, "I'm, er–" he glanced around cautiously – "looking for somebody. I have a little job and it's – um – not entirely above board, if you know what I mean."

"Oh yes?" Thorpe was interested. "As it happens,

I'm free at this time and a little job would be just up my street. You want someone dealt with?"

"Oh no," replied Gregory hurriedly. "Nothing like that, just a little redistribution of wealth."

Thorpe smiled. "You've come to the right man. I've just been dismissed from the police. Let's say I'm not enamoured with the law at the moment. And I know a bit about thefts."

Gregory looked shocked, feigning concern. "Really? So you'd drop me in it to get back into your boss's good books! Is that it?"

Thorpe grinned. "My boss would never trust me again, no matter what I did. No, friend; I'm looking for some easy money, and I suspect that a gent like you might have a good plan?"

"I know someone who is looking for a guard on a train, and I need to have that guard in my pocket."

"You need look no further, Mr, er–?"

"Gregory."

"Mr Gregory. I'm your man."

"Meet me here again next Thursday – same time." Gregory picked up his hat and left abruptly.

Thorpe watched him thoughtfully.

Later, when Gregory explained the details, Thorpe told him that the idea was clever, and he could not see how it could fail. To him, fifty pounds to look the other way for ten minutes on a train journey was very acceptable, especially as it would come on top of the pay for the guard duty offered by Sir Alexander.

"Better than a copper's salary," Gregory had expounded, and Thorpe had to agree.

Sir Alexander Wetherby was pleased to meet Thorpe when Gregory introduced the two men. Thorpe explained that he was a retired police sergeant and would be happy to take a relaxing train journey and look after the knight's luggage. He knew how most thieves worked and would be in a good position to prevent such a crime. After all, he pointed out, it was only an evening's light work for an experienced police officer.

In preparation, Gregory twice took a cab to Euston and travelled to Holyhead in order to work out a method of exchanging the jewellery. He carefully disguised himself both times. Some five days later, with Thorpe in place in the guard's van, minding Sir Alexander's luggage, Gregory boarded the Irish Mail. But Gregory had either never read, or he had forgotten, the immortal warning by Robert Burns: "The best-laid schemes o' mice an' men gang aft agley..."

CHAPTER 2

The Second Threads

Gordon Lowe, had he noticed the two young people gazing anxiously around on the platform, would doubtless have been surprised to find they had something in common with him. They too were concerned with parental anger. Unlike Mr Lowe's case, however, the pair were fleeing towards rather than away from a physical intimacy.

James Dixon was a personable young man with 'hopes in the City', according to his ambitious parents, even though his ambition lay in a different direction from theirs. Mr and Mrs Dixon had sent him to an expensive school, where a popular view in the staffroom was that his parents, if they were hoping for great things from their son, were wasting their money. He was well dressed, reasonably handsome, and could write clearly and spell with some accuracy, all of which were deemed satisfactory in a junior office clerk. His immediate superior had remarked to the departmental manager that if in the fullness of time young Dixon needed to be promoted to a more senior position, there should be no difficulty, always provided that he were given a competent secretary to ensure he did not embarrass the organisation.

Dixon, at the age of twenty-two, neither liked nor disliked his clerical work. He did not think about it much because he was in love. Some months ago in the office, he had glimpsed a pleasant-looking lady of middle years accompanied by a prettier and younger version of herself – presumably a daughter. This young lady had immediately attracted James' attention and interest, and he had listened as far as possible through an open door to her mother's conversation with his boss. The girl, introduced as Harriet, was eighteen years old, had just left school, and was visibly bored. She had gazed around the office as her mother, Mrs Thornton-Legge, discussed tedious business affairs.

Harriet caught a brief sight of James studying her and turned her head away quickly. A few moments later she glanced with lowered eyelids across at him again and saw him still watching her. She winked and James sighed in sudden delight as Cupid's arrow struck a bulls-eye in his heart. He smiled back at her, and the temptation for Cupid was too great to resist. Another arrow, this time to the lovely Harriet, was sent on its way.

Alea iacta est, the die had been cast.

After the pair left, James' normal, casual attitude to his job was pushed aside as he waited until his boss had a spare moment or two and approached him.

"Something I can do for you, Dixon?" the chief clerk enquired on seeing Dixon's approach.

"Er – yes, sir," Dixon hesitated. "Er – I was wondering..." He paused.

"Yes, you were wondering...?" The chief clerk waited, wondering himself at young Dixon producing evidence of mental activity.

"Um – the business you were discussing with that lady just now."

"Mrs Thornton-Legge? Yes. What was it you wanted to know?" Did the young clerk seriously have thoughts? This ought to be encouraged. But any thoughts Dixon may have searched for were proving evasive.

"I, er-, I–" he began, then miraculously an idea did occur – "I think I have seen the family."

"You have?" This was promising, thought the chief clerk. "In what connection?"

"Oh, er–" Dixon's brain reverted to its normal somnolent state. "Er – I cannot recall, sir."

"Well go back to your seat, Dixon, and return when you recollect what it is you wish to tell me." The chief clerk turned with regret back to his work. Pity, the lad had nearly used his brain then.

But there was indeed one firm intention that occupied the young man's mind deeply: he wanted to meet the young lady again, and get to know her better. His boss would have been very surprised had he known that James was forming a plan: he wanted Harriet's address. Once he had that, he could arrange to pass by as she left the house and possibly even – delightful thought – arrange to meet somewhere for a little chat.

Since that first happy day, James and Harriet secretly met at cafes on several occasions, and both had concluded that life without each other could not possibly be considered. In short, they planned to marry. There were only two difficulties: Harriet would need her parents' permission, and she knew that this would on no account be granted. The second problem concerned James' organisational ability: it didn't exist.

Fortunately, there was a solution to both hindrances. The blacksmith at Gretna Green in Scotland would solve one problem; he was renowned for conducting the marriages of couples too young to marry without parental permission in England. Harriet's native intelligence would obviate the other issue. James had, he had assured Harriet, sufficient money for the train fares; after that, well, their parents would surely not cut them off. Both had been to good schools and therefore, all things having been considered, life would be a breeze once they were married. They were both quite certain of that.

Once their decision had been made, Harriet had quickly sent James to purchase tickets at Euston in the late afternoon of their planned elopement date.

"Two third-class tickets to Gretna, please, on the next train to the north." James was nervous as he booked the tickets.

"The next train for Scotland will be tomorrow morning, sir. There's the mail train for Ireland leaving this evening, though," replied the smiling booking clerk. "But you'll need to change at Crewe, and again at Carlisle."

James had no idea where either place was, but since the clerk's words implied that they could get where they wanted to be that evening, he did not worry unduly. "Thank you," he said, grabbing the tickets and hurrying away.

The clerk glanced over to his colleague at the next counter. "My third couple this week, Jack," he chuckled. "What's your count so far?"

Harriet had told her parents she would be out visiting a girlfriend that evening; the girlfriend had been warned not to give the game away and deny any involvement. Harriet left the house and signalled a cab to take her to Euston Station, where she had arranged to meet James in the booking hall.

James hurried his would-be bride along the platform, glancing around nervously for any irate parents as he did so and then, seeing an empty compartment, he pointed to it saying, "There, my love, let's hop on quickly."

Harriet did as he had urged. "Yes, James, it looks comfortable, and we can sit and read something so that people passing by might not see us clearly."

She had surreptitiously packed a bag that afternoon and had left unaware that a chance remark of hers two days earlier had alerted her parents that something was afoot. They had considered the matter, presumed it had to do with that 'nice boy' she had mentioned more than once, and, knowing their daughter's intelligence and strong will, had hired a private detective agency to check on her activities. Harriet had not allowed for work by a detective agency and had not anticipated that someone would be standing behind James, listening as he bought the tickets.

The pair settled comfortably down in their compartment in quiet, pre-marital bliss, waiting for the train's departure.

***

The Harnsworth Detective Agency ('Trust us for results') was busy, and Reginald Harnsworth reluctantly passed the task of checking on the young lady over to Colin Hampton, who was rather slow, and not as eager for work as the manager wished his detectives to be. Consequently, the young pair in the train had no idea that they were being accompanied, albeit at a distance.

Mr Hampton settled down in a nearby compartment with his newspaper, relaxed in the knowledge that as soon as the train left he would have almost an hour and a half before he would need to check on the couple, when the train paused at Rugby. They would hardly be inclined to leap out at Tring or Bletchley as the train passed through at speed. He had left the house inadequately prepared for a long vigil. He really should have known better, he chided himself. Long, boring waits were very common in his job; the greenest young agent would have been better prepared, he admitted to himself.

Ah well, we all make the occasional error.

He noted too that he had omitted to pocket his pistol. He had never actually had to use it, but he was required to practise once a year on the agency's private range and was a reasonable shot, although he didn't know how he would react if things got tricky and he actually had to use it.

Well, there was no point in worrying about it now; he was already on the train. He might just as well visit the buffet car and spend half an hour enjoying a cup of coffee and a snack. Would a quick whisky be in order? Why not? One small snifter wouldn't affect his judgement. Alcohol was banned to those on duty, he knew, but how would the boss find out? He would be home again before anyone could smell his breath. It didn't even need to be a small one.

With these enticing thoughts, he left his seat in the direction of the buffet car.

He knew that their train was not bound for Scotland and that they would need to change at Crewe. He had anticipated that they would head for Gretna Green, like many other young hopefuls, and would need to change again; not all expresses for Glasgow stopped at Gretna. The couple would need to board a local train at Carlisle.

***

The ball at Count Montague Fitchworth's London residence had so far been a resounding success for the corpulent Lady Denise Marchant. Her husband, the late Sir Robert, had greatly obliged her by dying with a considerable estate intact before he could dispose of it through his pastime of gambling with the eager assistance of young single females at his London clubs. Now, Lady D believed, it was her turn to indulge. She had what she thought of as a voluptuous figure, including a magnificent bosom which she displayed to a fuller extent than was wise, even in high society. She hoped to attract the attention of eligible young men; nothing formal or lasting, you understand, but sufficient to provide a modicum of entertainment for a wealthy female of middle years and good breeding.

But the wide eyes among her intended observers, which she assumed to be caused by admiration, were actually registering disbelief. As she pirouetted and flirted with her dance partners, comments among observers watching from behind their fans revealed an interesting range of viewpoints.

"Has she seen a photograph of herself in that dress, I wonder?" mused the wife of a wealthy businessman to her neighbour the Countess of Neston. "I don't think Herbert has ever seen anything like that on his travels, not even in Tahiti!" Her husband had travelled to his connections all over the world.

"I fear," replied the Countess quietly, "that she might regret her choice of gown, should she not take great care."

"What a scandalous performance! Why was she invited to join civilised society?" hissed the Dowager

Duchess of Stafford.

"I say, Lady D is taking a major risk capering about like that, Joss. If she trips, her whole upper torso will be exposed to view," remarked young Lord Wilberforce to his companion, the Honourable Jocelyn Barchester.

"In Heaven's name, what was the Count thinking of, listing Lady Marchant among the guests?" The well-known stage actress Hermione Harrison was thought to have been one of the late King's lady visitors, and was hence acceptable into society.

Only one ancient Duke had anything remotely positive to say. "I must say that large female is showing great courage."

"That's not all she's showing, Father," his son, the Hon. Simon Throgmorton grumbled in reply. "I brought your grandson Alfred here tonight. I hope the sight doesn't put him off society. He's still very impressionable."

But far worse was to come. Lady Denise did indeed trip, as foreseen by young Lord W, but reached out and caught the arm of an astonished gentleman struggling to maintain his balance. However, as she used both arms to prevent herself from falling to the dance floor, she was no longer able to clutch at her décolleté to prevent the disaster which followed.

"Oops!" murmured the Hon. Jocelyn, while her partner tried without success to control his open laughter.

There was instant uproar, consisting largely of delight and hilarity from the younger attendees, with a small infusion of horror from the scandalised older female contingent.

A shawl was quickly proffered and wrapped around Lady Denise's shoulders as she was hurriedly escorted out to a dressing room.

On the way home in her cab, a furiously embarrassed Lady Denise came to a decision to leave London and return permanently to her stately home in Chorlton-cum-Hardy. Manchester society, she believed, would soon get over her disgrace (although she referred to it as a mishap), whereas London would scarcely allow her to forget it. She had already endured gossip in the past about Bob's well-known peccadilloes. Well, that would end. She would close down her London home and retire northwards. Tomorrow morning, she would instruct the staff to prepare for the move. Some would no doubt object, but they could either move with her or leave her employ; it was up to them.

By lunchtime the following day, her luggage had been packed and she had ordered her butler to contact an agent to dispose of her residence and remaining furniture and to keep her bank informed as to her finances. The butler had recommended a sleeping berth on a Manchester train on the Midland Railway from St Pancras, whereas on the Irish Mail she would need to change in Crewe in the middle of the night. However, the faster she could abandon London society, the happier she would be. The Irish Mail it was.

London society would regret its pathetic mirth at her unfortunate accident, she determined; although on hearing of her departure, much of that society breathed a sigh of relief.

A more conventionally dressed Lady Marchant strode haughtily along the platform at Euston, glaring around challenging anyone to make a comment on her appearance. No-one dared. She was followed by two porters, one struggling with her ladyship's outsized portmanteau and the other hauling a trolley loaded with her accompanying luggage. A uniformed platform official, seeing her approach, touched his cap and opened the door to a first-class compartment, indicating that she might like to enter.

She paused, gazed inside and, apparently satisfied, passed the man a florin and entered, leaving one porter to follow and place her portmanteau on the luggage rack and the other to wheel the trolley to the luggage van and see to its safe storage there. On his return to assure her that all was well, she handed him a guinea and instructed that it was to be shared with his colleague.

Settling down in her seat, Lady Marchant nodded over to the only other passenger in the compartment. His collar indicated he was a clerical gentleman. She was pleased: he would know nothing of her recent affairs and could not possibly embarrass her. He might even provide interesting conversation to pass the hours between Euston and Crewe.

"A very pleasant evening to you, sir." She nodded to him, smiling.

Canon Jones returned her smile with an internal grimace. "Indeed, madam, thank you." Hopefully she wasn't one of those women who wanted to chat and stop him reading his latest treasure, *The Importance of being Ernest*, an Oscar Wilde play.

He had covered the book with brown paper to hide its author's name; he admired Wilde but did not wish to broadcast his approbation for a man who had spent time in Reading Gaol for a crime which Canon Jones himself would willingly have committed had he dared. But his worries seemed to be short-lived as the lady took out a magazine and commenced to read.

***

Earlier that day, Fireman Johnny Winslowe had stared at the enginemen's list in Camden locomotive shed in sheer delight: his dearest wish appeared to have been granted. He and his driver, Patrick O'Leary, were to take the down Irish Mail as far as Crewe again that night but this time, instead of one of the older locomotives they were used to, they had one of Mr Bowen-Cooke's brand-new powerful express passenger locomotives: a Claughton class, no less! Johnny had seen several of these new engines built for the heavily loaded trains to Crewe or Carlisle, and had been hoping to be able to fire one soon. Tonight, he would indeed be firing one, with

Mr O'Leary on the regulator. They would come off at Crewe with just over two hours' break, before returning to Euston with the up Mail. Their own engine would probably come off the train at Crewe and be replaced for the rest of the North Wales run to Holyhead. All in all, a straightforward seven- or eight-hours' duty.

But his good mood was dampened when he saw the grim look on his driver's face. "Something wrong, Mr O'Leary? You don't look to be your cheerful self, today."

"It's another letter from me sister in Kilkenny, Johnny. She writes that our parents are unwell an' she can't help 'em as much as they need. She has her own four kids ter look after and she 'as ter help on the farm. Our da broke his leg last week and our mam is now bedridden. I may have ter go back to Ireland quicker than I expected." In his disappointment, the driver's Irish brogue was stronger than usual.

"Oh." Johnny was also disappointed. Patrick O'Leary had been his regular driver for almost ten years now, and the two men had formed an impressive team. Johnny was an efficient fireman, much appreciated by Driver O'Leary, and the latter was easily the best driver Johnny had ever been paired with. He gave plenty of valuable advice, which Johnny had taken to heart, and he was an entertaining companion, if occasionally tempted into a leg-pull.

"Can't be helped, Johnny, me boy. Yer a good lad

an' ye'll make a damn good driver one day soon. I'll be thinkin' of ye when I'm driving in Ireland, so I will. Now let's go an' have a look at our engine, an' get 'er ready for the run."

They walked over to their big locomotive waiting on a siding in the late afternoon sun, gleaming in her new blackberry-black paint.

"She looks a real picture, Mr O'Leary," commented Johnny as they approached.

"Aye, she does, but she'll want preparin', so let's get at 'er," replied his driver.

Large express locomotives needed plenty of preparation time before they had enough steam to take on a train, and the enginemen would be busy for an hour or so. The shed staff had already spent a couple of hours on getting her fire ready and her tender filled with water and suitable coal. As a rule, the railway companies supplied high quality coal for passenger trains; passengers were quicker to complain about late trains, whereas coal, iron ore and general merchandise were less inclined to grumble.

The driver would go round with his oil-can and lubricate the motion, coupling rods and so on, while the fireman would check the fire, filling up any gaps. Then he would check the water gauges and steam pressure, which would need to be brought up sufficiently so that the driver had enough power for what was needed. Finally, he would sweep the cab, removing any coal or grit that might cause an engineman to slip while on duty.

The two men went through these duties automatically; they each knew that they could rely on the other not to take any shortcuts which might reflect badly on the engine's performance during the run. By eight-thirty in the evening, they could relax over a mug of tea and a sandwich in the cab before they took their engine to Euston and backed onto their train, ready for the long haul to Crewe.

Fireman Winslowe had to climb down from the cab to the track to couple the engine to its train. The heavy link, which had to take the weight of more than 300 tons, had to be lifted and dropped over the hook on the front coach. Then the screw had to be tightened sufficiently to prevent undue flexibility between engine and train. Annoying vibration was another feature of railway travel provoking letters of complaint to be written and sent to the company.

Finally, the steam heating and brake vacuum pipes needed to be connected in order that heating could be supplied through the train and the cab crew could brake the whole train, rather than just the locomotive.

As Johnny was climbing back into the cab, the guard came up, calling to the driver. "You've got ten on today, Patrick, three-fifty tons," he called.

"Thanks, Herb, and anything special?"

"No, nothing to worry about this time, Pat. Should be a straightforward run." Guard Herbert Simmons turned to walk back to his van at the rear of the train.

"Looks like we'll have an easy three-an'-a-half-hours to Crewe, Johnny." Patrick smiled at his fireman as he waited for the starting signal to drop and the green flag from the guard as soon as the train was ready to depart. "A break in Crewe, then the same back. Should be a relaxing day's duty." But Driver O'Leary's optimism, like that of his passenger Gregory, was unwarranted.

The two enginemen were slightly anxious in preparing their steed for the steep climb up Camden Bank. Euston Station had been built in 1837 for the London and Birmingham Railway, and the initial ascent out of London had been too steep for the locomotives of the day, so the first trains leaving Euston had been assisted by a cable for the initial half-dozen years. After 1844, a pilot locomotive had been attached to trains to assist them with the climb. But with a reasonable load and a brand-new locomotive, Patrick believed that assistance was not needed; their Claughton should be able to manage easily.
  "Righto, Johnny me boy, now we're goin' to find out what these big engines are made of," he chortled. "I've bin lookin' forward to getting' me hands on one. The lads who've driven 'em say they're the bees' knees."
  "I hope they're right, Mr O'Leary. I've heard very positive things about them too. But I've also heard that they are heavy on coal as well, so I'm not sure I'm looking forward to the trip as much as you are."

CHAPTER 3

The Tangles begin

The starter signal at the end of the platform dropped and Johnny called out, "We've got the starter, Mr O'Leary."

Next, he looked back to the rear of the train to see the guard waving his green flag, "And Guard Simmons has given us the green."

"Right, ye are then Johnny, let's see what she's made of." Driver O'Leary released the engine brake and eased the regulator gently upwards. The locomotive moved off slowly and smoothly with apparent ease as Johnny fired around the firebox to build up the steam pressure enough for his driver to be able to tackle the Camden Bank without embarrassing them.

As their train snaked through the points and crossings outside the station, Patrick began to build up speed on the long straight section with the blasts from the chimney returning an echo from the long rows of terraced houses on both sides of the main line up towards Camden Junction. The ten heavy coaches of the Mail train did not appear to worry their engine as they accelerated up the long bank. They passed a rake of suburban coaches being hauled down into to Euston by a small tank engine ready to form a local train for Watford Junction or Bletchley.

Johnny pointed to it, remarking, "That was my first job as a sprog fireman on the passenger link, Mr O'Leary. I had Driver Hepton showing me the ropes."

"Bill Hepton? Didn't like the man meself, but I hear he wasn't a bad driver, even if a bit surly in his cab."

"He was not that bad when you get used to his ways." Johnny changed the subject. He hadn't much enjoyed his time with Driver Hepton but didn't want to spread any gossip. Driver Hepton had involved himself in some dubious activity with his guard; they had been bribed by a district judge to provide a prostitute for him on a train journey, and both railwaymen had been dismissed from the service.

"When d'you think you'll be leaving to go back to help your parents?" Johnny's mind moved back to the topic in hand.

"As soon as I can get meself a drivin' job in Ireland with the Great Southern and Western Railway. They've written askin' for a recommendation from the North-Western here, an' they'll let me know when they've got one. So it might be a fair while yet."

Johnny had always relished his trips with Patrick and deeply regretted that they would end soon. He had no doubt at all that the L&NWR would give his driver a good reference; Patrick O'Leary was one of the best drivers in Camden Shed, as most would readily agree. In the meantime, he would enjoy what little time he had left with his Irish driver. The man had become a good friend and a mentor as well.

Half an hour later, Johnny gazed out of the cab as they left the brief stop at Watford Junction. Their engine was steaming easily and effortlessly; Driver O'Leary had her well in hand.

***

By the time the train had passed Wembley an elegant young lady, Mrs Edna Clayton, had finally settled herself down and replaced her bag on the luggage rack after she had taken out her ticket ready for inspection. She had arrived in the train in something of a hurry and had spent the intervening minutes checking her luggage.

That morning, her husband Jonathon had insisted on travelling separately but had not told her very many details about what he was planning. He had not explained whether they would be returning the following day and she had forgotten to ask, so she had not understood exactly how much to pack. Should she pack nightwear, for instance? Consequently, she had been checking whether she had enough clothing for all eventualities.

She now looked around her. There were three other passengers in her compartment and she nodded to them with a smile. The older married couple sitting together greeted her with a polite "Good evening, miss."

The other gentleman; a man in his early forties, she

estimated, doffed his hat to her and bowed his head while remaining seated. Despite his apparent manners, he had a gleam in his eye which Edna recognised immediately. This man fancied her, and he would need watching, but as long as there were others in their compartment, she would not need to take any action. If the couple left, that would be a very different matter, but she had no fears even if that were the case. She could deal with it by means of a call for help, unless the issue became more urgent, in which case her hatpin should work nicely. It wouldn't be the first time.

Her husband was in the first-class carriage, near the luggage van at the rear of the train. She had no particular role, Jonathon had told her, but she might be useful in case any distraction was needed at some stage between Euston and Holyhead.

Distraction? she had thought at the time. Yes, she was good at that. Where men were concerned, she would have no problem in quickly thinking up something. She knew men, and she knew that even those who believed themselves to be gentlemen had lechery hidden deep in their systems. Some were even unaware of it.

But Jonathon Gregory had made a rare error on this occasion: he had not seen the need to inform his wife that his jewellery advisor Smeddle was also on the train. Nor had he introduced Smeddle to his wife, believing that the more others knew about the details of his plans, the more likely those details were to fall into the wrong hands. 'Trust nobody' was his motto, and the 'nobody' included his nearest and dearest – although 'dearest' expressed an emotion with which he was completely unfamiliar. He regarded his wife with pride rather than undying love. She was both decorative and intelligent and was a visible demonstration of his social success. His peace of mind about her was undisturbed because he was unaware that there were one or two male members in his own social group who were very familiar with the delectable Mrs Clayton, having availed themselves of her services from time to time. These clients of Edna's who knew Jonathon were extremely careful to ensure that he had no inkling of their relationship with his wife. They knew they were treading on very thin ice indeed, but the rewards were worth it; Edna provided pleasures that were out of this world. They knew they were living dangerously, but as long as they were living, the game was worth the candle.

These abilities of his wife's were the sole reason Edna was important to Jonathon. For him, such feelings as affection and love were totally foreign and therefore possibly hazardous diversions. This mistake was most unfortunate because the man opposite Edna, with the dishonourable glint in his eye, was none other than his jeweller, Henry Smeddle himself.

Although he assured himself that he was a happily married man, Smeddle had no compunction in occasionally treating himself to a little extra-marital entertainment. Even the late King Edward VII himself... Smeddle's thoughts abandoned monarchs and their peccadilloes as he eyed the charming young lady across the compartment. He spent a diverting half-hour thinking about what he could do with that tempting creature, should the occasion present itself. Possibly even before they arrived in Crewe? Perhaps he could somehow lure her into a toilet and then...?

His mind began to work rapidly and move into areas of delightful fantasy. All at once he had a brainwave: he could offer her one of the jewels he had brought to exchange with Sir Whatzisname's collection! What luscious young thing did not, um... lower her defences when presented with such a pretty bauble? First, he would place it on a necklace, and she would allow him to hang it round her neck, and then, when she was busily admiring the effect in the mirror, he would start to undo the buttons down her...

Such thoughts entranced him for several minutes while he stared blankly out of the window at the last few passengers boarding the train under the platform lights as they waited for last doors to slam and the train to gently move off. Smeddle relaxed, his eyes partially closed, as the train made its way out of Euston, accelerating through Camden. By the time they passed Carpenders Park, they were racing out of London and on their way north. He had his fingers crossed that the older couple might alight in Rugby and nobody would enter their compartment, leaving him alone with his young companion.

***

The urgent need for eluding her parents and obtaining a cab for Euston had been very tiring for a young girl unused to such devious planning, so once the train had moved off Harriet had drifted into a light sleep, leaning gently on James' shoulder. He too was completely relaxed. Here he was with this beautiful girl leaning on him and trusting him, on his way to marry her with no 'let or hindrance', as it stated in a document he had once seen. Exactly what that meant he was unsure, but it sounded comforting. They were on their way to wedded bliss and nothing would now stop them. He was totally at ease with himself when the compartment door slid open as a man in uniform looked in.

"Tickets please, ladies and gentlemen," Guard Herbert Simmons announced. The passengers fumbled in their bags and pockets, producing their tickets. The guard clipped them and, looking at James' ticket with a smile, said, "You'll need to change into a Glasgow express at Crewe, sir, and change again into a local train at Carlisle for Gretna."

On hearing this, there were poorly disguised smiles from one or two of the other passengers.

James nodded his thanks. He had no idea where either Crewe or Carlisle were, but he would see the platform signs when they got there. The guard shut the door again, wondering why the young couple had not booked directly onto a Carlisle train but then grinned, recalling that when he was young he and

Shirl had married only seven months before their son had been born. Had these two also been a tad careless, and now in a hurry to get hitched before any evidence of their premature dalliance could publicly accuse them?

In the meantime, with his bride-to-be leaning trustingly on his shoulder, James stared out of the darkening window at the figures and lights passing with increasing speed before his eyes. He felt totally at ease.

The sliding door woke Harriet and James gazed at her. "Can I get you a cup of tea or something to eat?" he asked tenderly. "I'm sure there will be a buffet on the train somewhere."

"No food thank you, James, but a cup of tea would be very welcome."

James nodded and left the compartment to look for the buffet car. He returned fifteen minutes later, carrying two cups, and was surprised to see that Harriet had laid a small cloth with a plate of sandwiches on his seat.

"Something I prepared before leaving home," she explained. "I thought we might be in a hurry and we need to save money anyway."

James was delighted, "Attagirl!" How had he managed to snare such a gem?

After they had consumed the sandwiches, Harriet packed everything neatly away and sat back to lean on James' shoulder again. James took out a book someone had given him. He had intended to follow the advice his boss had once offered, to 'take up some high-minded reading', and this journey north offered a good opportunity to begin. It might even endear him further to his future bride, he hoped. She would certainly approve of this urge to improve his mind. He looked at the title: *Three Men in a Boat*. Ah, a technical book! He might be able to learn more about boat handling. He had not been a great success at school in the rowing team; his habit of falling overboard had not endeared him to his team-mates. Perhaps reading this book might show him what he had not fully understood. Mr Jerome's treatise might prove of great value to him. James settled down to study how to improve his marine skills.

***

In a first-class compartment nearer the front of the train, Lady Marchant finished her magazine, dropped it on the empty seat beside her, and stared at her sole companion, who was quietly reading his book. As she was about to open a conversation with the unsuspecting man, the door slid open and the guard entered.

"Tickets, please, madam. And you, sir."

Both passengers found their tickets and held then out to be clipped.

"I understand that I will need to change trains in Crewe. Is that correct, my man?"

The automatic arrogance in Lady Marchant's voice and manner was designed to inform Guard Simmons that he was dealing with the aristocracy, but Herbert Simmons was well used to handling those who felt themselves to be superior to the rest of humanity.

"Quite correct, madam. A Manchester train will be leaving Crewe shortly after we arrive. You may want to request a porter for assistance. The Manchester train will be leaving from a different platform, as I am sure you are aware." *We menials have our uses*, he thought. He clipped the canon's ticket with a "Goodnight."

Lady Marchant looked over at the canon once again. A man of the church; she had noted his white collar with approval on entering the train and now she leaned forward to tap him on the knee. It was time the man showed a little civility to his distinguished female traveller.

"We shall be travelling together for some hours, I presume, sir. I consider it behoves us to be polite to one another. May I introduce myself? Lady Denise Marchant of Chorlton, near Manchester. You are, I take it from your garb, a man of the cloth?"

Canon Jones looked up in surprise. Wilde's book was highly entertaining, although not quite what he had hoped for; his mind had gradually turned to sinful fantasies about that new young Anglican priest in Llandudno, when he was brought back suddenly to the present.

"Oh, er–certainly, madam." He stood up and bowed briefly. "Canon Glyn Jones of Deganwy."

"Deganwy," Lady Marchant said thoughtfully. "I do not know of this town. Pray inform me of its location."

"It lies on the North Wales coast between Llandudno Junction and Llandudno, Lady Marchant."

He hoped she wasn't planning to engage him in conversation. His private fantasy had been pleasantly distracting.

"I do not see the title of the book you are perusing." Lady Marchant spoke with what she hoped was an encouraging smile. (The canon would have classified it as a grimace.) Was the wretched woman going to chat all the way to Crewe, where she would presumably change trains and allow him an hour and a half's peace to continue his fantasy about the young priest? A quite different thought occurred to him and he took pleasure in informing her of the title of his reading matter. "I am reading *The Importance of being Ernest*, madam. It is a play by Oscar Wilde. You may have heard of him."

"Oscar Wilde?" There was a distinct note of disapproval in her tone. "Was he not put into prison for some crime or other?"

"Indeed he was, Lady Marchant." Would that stop her? *Let's pile it on.* "He served two years in Reading Gaol."

"I see." Lady Marchant sniffed then picked up her magazine and began to study it once more.

Excellent! That had shut her up. Problem solved, thought the canon.

He also picked up his book and started to read again where he had left off some minutes ago. All at once he stopped, stared at Lady Marchant, coughed, and rapidly left the compartment.

"Do excuse me for a moment, madam," he gasped as he hurried out into the corridor. He moved away along the corridor well out of earshot from their compartment and began to laugh uncontrollably. He had just come across Lady Bracknell's description of Miss Prism: 'An elderly female person of repellent aspect'. He had been sitting opposite exactly such a female for the last half-hour! He would have to tell the young priest about this.

It took another ten minutes to bring himself under control again, and then he re-entered the compartment. Now he would hopefully be able to sit, read, and engage in his private fantasies without disturbance for a couple of hours.

He sat back in his seat and his mind immediately went to the young priest.

***

Elsewhere in the train, Jeff Waterman and Thumper Dawson had quite different worries. Thumper was sitting in a compartment in the same coach as Lowe while Waterman was standing just outside the same compartment, from where he could keep an eye on Lowe (and on Thumper, who needed to be watched much of the time). He was trying to work out how they could get Lowe to enter a toilet where he could be thoroughly but quietly sorted out, yet leave Thumper and himself a simple and speedy getaway before authority, with serious medical assistance, could be called in. This would have to be done a few minutes before they were due to arrive at a station where they could quickly detrain and disappear. Thumper would need no more than three minutes, judging by previous experience.

Waterman knew that there were few stops on this train, the first being at Rugby in over an hour. Then there was Crewe, and after Crewe only Chester before Holyhead. He had checked the times and recalled something he had seen in the timetable. Hmm – there was a longish break between Chester and Holyhead. Perhaps something could be organised between the two? Chuck the bloke out of the train in the dark? No, that would be murder for sure, and they hadn't murdered anyone yet – although that old docker who had been pilfering his lordship's—

But his heart attack had been three weeks later, Waterman told himself. No, even Thumper might draw the line at topping someone. Then there would be the problem of getting away quickly: no stop until Holyhead. No, that wouldn't do. It would be best before Crewe or Chester.

Thumper himself, on the other hand, was concerned with more urgent matters. *Where the 'ell 'ave I put me knuckledusters? In an assignment wivout 'em last year I'd ripped a fingernail orf an' it 'ad fuckin' well 'urt! What if I 'urt meself agen; where would that leave us? I wouldn't be able ter belt anyone! Also, wot are we goin' to do abaht me belly? Jeff 'asn't mentioned anyfing about any tea. I couldn't do me duty on an empty belly an' it's begun to rumble already. Why 'asn't Jeff done somefing about getting' our grub? If fings don't 'appen soon, I'm goin' ter 'ave ter smack somebody.*

Thumper was a worried man.

***

At the front of the train, Driver O'Leary and Fireman Winslowe had no such worries. As they raced through Bletchley and then Wolverton, it was clear that their big Claughton had the train well in hand. Patrick was obviously enjoying himself on the left-hand side of the cab, with his hand on the regulator and his eyes on the signals; not always as easy to pick up in the night sky as one might imagine. Johnny was relieved to discover that the locomotive was not quite as heavy on coal as he had been led to believe. He was thinking that if the job was as easy as this on the way back in the morning, it would be a pleasant duty altogether. But both he and Patrick were in total ignorance of a major change in their arrangements for duty which would be waiting for them on their arrival in Crewe.

As they raced on smoothly through the dark night, both men were beginning to enjoy driving and firing this powerful locomotive which seemed to have no limit to its power. It promised to be a shift which put pure pleasure into driving a steam locomotive. The engine was master of its train, the coal was keeping the fire at the right heat for maintaining steam pressure and not too demanding on the fireman's arms and shoulders; at least, felt Johnny, not so far. Patrick too was clearly in his element, standing at the regulator and gazing out of the cab spectacle plate, watching for the signals and reacting to their demands. Even the signalmen in the signal cabins were playing their part as if they knew that the crew with their big engine were not to be delayed – which of course was true.

Forty minutes after leaving Euston, Patrick leaned over to call to Johnny: "I like these Claughtons, Johnny. I'll be sorry not to continue driving 'em, so I will. The GS&WR have some big locos, but they're only freight engines and I'm told they are rough riders and have a tendency to fall off the rails, so I'm not looking forward to any fancy drivin'."

"Well, you never know, Mr O'Leary, they might be planning to build better engines very soon."

"Aye, I've heard that too, me boy. I hope it's true. But there is one problem I still have to solve here in England."

"And that is?"

"Ye're not yet a driver."

Johnny laughed, "That'll be years yet."

But Patrick was serious. "No, I mean it, Johnny. Ye've the makin's of a grand driver. I've given ye the regulator more'n once an' ye know what ye're doin'."

Patrick O'Leary had often allowed his fireman to drive for short periods and had no qualms at letting him do so when there was no danger of a senior officer catching sight of them, particularly now, as they raced through the dark night. No platform inspector or signalman in his cabin could see who was driving as they passed at speed. It was in fact common practice among drivers who felt they could trust their firemen to drive for a time, and Patrick knew Johnny was already a competent, if as yet unacknowledged, driver.

The fireman paused and then said slowly, "I was going to tell you later this week. I've been studying the rules for a while and applied for the test. They've told me it'll be early next month."

Patrick's face lit up in delight. "Did ye, begorrah?! Well, ye can practise again today, so ye can. Ye're on the regulator for 'alf an hour after we leave Rugby, an' ye'll drive as if 'twas Himself on yer tail! An' when ye're a full driver, I'll be happy goin' back to me parents again, so I will!"

CHAPTER 4

Rebellion at Rugby

"The cups!" James Dixon suddenly recalled. He had been specifically asked to return them to the buffet car. In his pleasure at finding Harriet's sandwiches, he had completely forgotten them. He gently removed Harriet's dozing head from his shoulder and arose, picking up the cups from the adjacent seat and leaving the compartment with them. As he walked through the corridor, he passed the compartment containing Edna Clayton, and the two exchanged brief glances.

Good heavens, what a beauty! he mused, then chided himself as he recalled the purpose of his journey with Harriet. What on earth was he doing, eyeing up other pretty girls? He was on his way to get married, for Heaven's sake! He had no need whatsoever to admire other young ladies when he was in the company of the girl he expected to make his wife, thus demonstrating his abysmal ignorance of a major feature of masculinity.

Edna also noticed the young man passing in the corridor. She did not chide herself. *Hmm, I'd rather have that handsome lad chatting me up than this loathsome creature in the opposite seat,* she considered idly; *or, for that matter, my husband. Jonathon's a good catch, no doubt about it, but he's no fun in bed.* Edna's mental language slid briefly back into her Piccadilly street-girl days, *An' if that randy young bugger Jeffrey Attwood, Jonathon's mate, rips me draws orf agen like 'e did last month, when Jonathon was on 'is trip to Holy'ead, I'll tell Jonathon what 'e done ter me an' 'e'll sort the bastard aht. Nah, that docker – wot was 'is nime? Hendrik? Well, some foreign moniker any'ow.* (He had been a regular customer in her Piccadilly days.) *'E giv real value fer money, 'e did. 'E knew wot a girl like me wanted and giv it regular and wiv some umph!* Then she noticed how her thoughts were worded, recalled who she was now supposed to be, and amended her silent language immediately.

She frowned as she watched the middle-aged couple standing up and checking their luggage. It looked as if they might be leaving the train shortly, at Rugby. This could mean that she would be alone with Lecherous Len over there for two hours before they reached Crewe. Then there was that longer non-stop section between Chester and Holyhead. She had a very good idea of exactly how it would proceed. He would start a conversation and offer her something, followed by a swift move to sit next to her, and before much longer his hands would be everywhere on her person. She knew the type well.

Should she move? Go to see Jonathon? Pull out her hatpin in a threatening manner? Such thoughts circled in her brain until she decided to wait until Rugby and see whether the beast would make a move. If he did then she would react accordingly.

Some of Smeddle's considerations mirrored Edna's. He had also noticed the preparations of the other couple and assumed they were intending to leave at Rugby. It was quite possible that no-one else would enter the compartment, leaving him with this innocent young creature at his mercy. Once the ticket-collector had checked all the entraining passengers' tickets, there would be two hours during which most passengers would be asleep.

Plenty of time to set up a cordial chat, followed by an amusing little ten-minute interlude – perhaps in the toilet, where they would not be disturbed? Surely Gregory would not want to act just yet; the best time for the theft and Smeddle's participation would obviously be closer to Holyhead, around one-thirty or two in the morning? There was plenty of time for a little amusement.

Smeddle returned to his book after straightening his tie and trying a wink at Edna, which she ignored. He quickly rubbed his eye to try and pretend that he had not winked at her. *So, she's playing 'hard to get'*, he thought. No matter, she wasn't the first he had mellowed; she just needed patient handling. He began to think about other means that he had employed in past situations to persuade young ladies to see things his way. He was optimistic, as he had not often been refused; this time he just needed to choose a suitably effective approach. He would consider this while he waited for the couple to actually leave the train. He would then wait until the ticket collector had checked the compartment and as long as no other passengers had entered and occupied the vacant seats, he could begin his attempted seduction.

He sat with a gentle smile on his face, staring out of the window at the passing bushes and trees lit by the light from the carriage windows.

Should further passengers enter the compartment, then he could wait until the girl left to visit the toilet and he would follow a minute or two later; females often took longer in such visits than men were inclined to do. His actions would not look suspicious to the casual observer. The other people might even be asleep and none the wiser anyway. One should always look on the bright side – a cliché, no doubt, but worth considering.

***

Edna's husband, in the meantime, left his seat and went to check on Thorpe, to see that the ex-policeman was actually on duty on the train. Sir Alexander had been very grateful to Gregory for supplying the name of a former police sergeant. Naturally, neither Gregory nor Thorpe had indicated why the latter was no longer in the force.

The aristocrat had agreed with Gregory that he sounded an ideal person to act as a guard.

Gregory walked through the train to the luggage van at the rear. Passengers were not allowed inside, of course, but there was a convenient window through which he could see that all seemed to be in order. Thorpe was sitting reading a paper, and Gregory tapped gently on the window. Thorpe looked up, saw Gregory, and nodded at him, indicating with a gesture that all was under control.

Gregory nodded in return, pleased that his choice of assistant had worked out so well. An ex-copper with a probable grudge against his former employers was almost certainly an excellent candidate for his proposed plan. He knew the scheme was a good one, with a high chance of success. Thorpe himself had a definite air of quiet competence and showed none of the concern that Gregory had sometimes detected in Smeddle, for instance. No, Thorpe was a man who Gregory felt he could use again in the future, as long as the present arrangement had proved successful – not that he had any doubts that it would.

With these notions in his mind, he returned to check that Edna also had boarded the train. He came along the corridor, saw her reading, and stopped short. She did not see him, and he caught a brief sight of the older couple, but missed that his own man Smeddle was opposite her in the compartment. The older man had stood up to reach and pull down his suitcase and so obscured Gregory's view, which was extremely unfortunate. He would otherwise have noticed Smeddle, and perhaps introduced Edna to the jeweller. This omission was to have most regrettable consequences.

***

Gordon Lowe was very uneasy in his seat. The compartment had four other passengers and only one seat was vacant. He had found – fortunately, he thought – a place next to the window on the corridor side so that he could keep an eye out for possible trouble. So far there had been nothing obvious, but you never knew, and it paid to be ready to scarper, but there was one problem: where could one scarper to on a damn train?

Rugby was the next stop so perhaps he should get ready to leave there, or would it be better to put more distance between himself and London first? Money was not a problem; he had plenty of readies in his pocket. What about Crewe? Not much of place; nobody would think of looking there, and anyway from a big junction like Crewe he could catch a train to anywhere. That would keep Lord bloody Edale guessing! He could then find somewhere to stay until the fuss in London had completely died down and return quietly to a different house and a new name. It wouldn't be hard to organise.

Even so, he mused to himself, he had been a little careless with that Rosy. He really ought to have checked her out first before slipping her that Mickey

Finn. Mind you, she had seemed willing enough.

Crewe then, he decided, his mind returning to the scene at hand. Until then, sit tight and keep your eyes peeled! He took a newspaper from his pocket and opened it up, thus hiding most of his upper torso and face from any passing observers; not that there would be many on an overnight train.

He was not to know that Messrs Waterman and Dawson were less than five yards away and were very interested in his wellbeing, with a view to thoroughly compromising it.

***

"Listen, Thumper," said Waterman to his companion, "we need to wait until after Rugby when he'll want to go to the toilet. We'll follow him there and then when he opens the door you can push him right in. I'll stand outside and keep watch."

"Gotcher!" replied Thumper. "An' when 'e's inside?"

"Why, then you'll have a word with him."

"A word wiv me iron fist!" Thumper added in triumph. He had discovered his knuckledusters under his cap. For some reason, officers of the law had taken to patting him down on sight in London's streets. He didn't know why but had taken to keeping his work tools up under his hat because the coppers didn't seem to search there.

"I don't know why the coppers always check me pockets, Jeff," he said. "Every time we go aht inter the streets the bastards check me pockets. Why, fer Christ's sake?"

Waterman smiled at his mate. It was difficult to resist the odd tease from time to time with Thumper. "Don't you know?"

"O' course not. How should I know?"

"Could it be that picture of you in the cop shops whenever we are asked to visit, d'you think?"

"I s'pose. But why 'ave they got me mugshot all over the place?"

"Might it be because when I'm not with you, you have a tendency to hit people?"

"Yeah, but fair dos, Jeff; that's on'y cos they won't give me money when I asks 'em."

Waterman extended the tease with a tricky question. "What if you ask me for money and I don't give you any more?"

Thumper puzzled over this for a moment then smiled. "But you're me mate."

Waterman gave up. "Look, just don't hit people unless I tell you to."

"If yer ses so, Jeff."

Waterman changed the topic. "Good. Now let's go and find the bloke."

"What bloke?"

Waterman sighed. "The bloke his lordship's asked us to see."

"Ah!" Thumper smiled in anticipation. "That bloke. The bloke wot 'e wants doin' over?"

Thankful that they now had that sorted, Waterman eased carefully along the corridor to check once more on their quarry. He was still sitting by the window, and Waterman stopped short of the compartment again, where Lowe could not see him.

"There he is, Thumper. Don't let him see us. We'll wait back a bit until he gets up."

"When's 'e goin' ter the bog?"

Waterman was startled. "How the hell should I know? When he has to, I imagine."

Thumper noticed a reduction in the train's speed. "Ey up, we're goin' ter stop. 'E can't go fer a piss now; it's not allowed."

This unexpected assertion surprised Waterman. "How do you know that?"

"I seen it somewhere."

Waterman shook his head; he couldn't fathom how his friend's mind worked on the admittedly rare occasions when it did.

***

Finally, Lowe noticed Waterman had been standing outside his compartment for a while and it set his nerves on edge.

As the train slowed down on entering Rugby Station, a few passengers began to gather in the corridors with their hands on the doors. The train stopped gently, a few doors were opened, and passengers began to disembark before others started to board, as soon as the doorways were free.

A portly gentleman with a large suitcase eased himself past Waterman, muttering, "Pardon me, sir."

Waterman, surprised at being addressed as 'sir' was nonplussed for a moment and distracted. At this exact moment, Lowe scrambled out of his seat and made for the door, pushing past two other passengers. He dropped out of the train and began to hurry along the platform, looking for an exit. Waterman leaped after him, calling to Thumper as he did so. Thumper once roused was a man not to be trifled with and he hurried along the corridor in the train, on the trail of his mate and their quarry.

***

Patrick O'Leary looked at Johnny. "As soon we've left the station and are out of the suburbs, Johnny, you can have the regulator for a spell."

"Thanks, Mr O'Leary. I'm looking forward to it. But I'm glad you're waiting until after Rugby; there's one problem here I always find a bit difficult."

"Oh, what's that then?"

"It's that signal gantry on the approaches. I've often tried to count the number of signals on it and never managed it!"

"Oh aye, 'tis a grand gantry and no mistake. I've had to slow down meself once or twice to check which signal's for the down main."

The signal gantry at Rugby stretched across all the tracks and was often commented on by drivers and fireman; it contained a huge array of signals. This could easily confuse enginemen, especially if the weather was foggy. Many drivers had complained to the railway company but so far nothing had been done to ease the problem. However, on this occasion the lights were clear and Patrick slowed the train down to a gentle stop. There were not too many passengers at this time of night and the porters had little to do.

"We'll be off again sooner than I would have thought," remarked Patrick as he glanced along the platform and saw the guard standing with his green flag under his arm, ready to wave them off. But there was a sudden commotion as a man jumped out of the train and ran along the platform, followed by another man who was clearly chasing him.

"What the hell?' muttered Patrick as he watched the incident. The first man jumped back into the train as the second leaped after him and a nearby grinning porter slammed the door shut behind them both and waved to the guard that all was well. The guard nodded and waved his flag. Patrick grasped the regulator and eased the train gently away again. The incident had not held them up at all.

"What was all that?" asked Johnny as he picked up his shovel to begin firing.

"No idea, Johnny. Some cove jumped out of the train, was chased by another, and they both hopped back in again. The guard gave his 'all clear', so off we went."

Johnny nodded, thinking that if he was going to drive soon he had better make sure the fire was ready. He didn't want his driver to be able to criticise his preparation, nor did he want to suffer because his own fire wasn't adequate for what he would require for the next half-hour or so when he was driving. He checked once more, put another ten shovelfuls round the firebox, and checked again. Yep, that would do.

Once they had passed the main line junction where the route to Birmingham branched off on their left, Patrick nodded over to Johnny. "Righto, Johnny me lad, she's all yours for a spell." He moved to the right in the cab and held his hand out for the shovel. Johnny passed it over, took hold of the regulator, and settled himself down on the little seat to gaze out of the window. The view from the front spectacle plate allowed him to see the signals. Although he felt a slight nervousness, it soon passed. This was something he had done many times before, although never for half an hour at a stretch, and never in one of these new express passenger engines. Patrick's trust in him was very comforting.

***

In the train, however, comfort was the last thing on Lowe's mind; Waterman had nearly caught him as he had leaped back onboard. As he had been racing away, he had seen the guard opening his flag ready to signal to the driver that the train was ready to depart. He had decided that he could jump back into the train, leaving his pursuer stuck and swearing on the platform while he got away.

There was a heavier fellow waiting by the door with

a grin on his face and holding his hand out to help him back in.

"Thank you, sir!" Lowe gasped as he reached for the man's outstretched hand. But the grin on the large fellow's face grow broader as Lowe's pursuer, who must have also jumped back on board, reached them. Lowe had a feeling that his apparent escape was looking more like a trap.

The large fellow let go of Lowe's hand in order to seize his arm in a firm grip. "Was yer goin' somewhere?" asked the fellow.

Lowe felt the man's grasp like a tight band of iron round his arm. He wasn't going anywhere, it seemed.

"I, er – I just needed a spot of fresh air," he muttered.

The grin broadened even further. "Did yer, now?"

Just then an angel of rescue appeared, heavily disguised as Herbert Simmons, the train guard. "Anything wrong here, gentlemen?"

He had hurried through the train to find out what all the commotion had been about.

Waterman intervened. "Not at all. We thought we saw this gentleman slide out of the train door and we wanted to help him back into his seat." He turned his attention to Lowe. "This here was your seat, I believe, sir," he said, pointing to where Lowe had been sitting previously.

Lowe nodded, speechless. He didn't know what else to do. "Thank you," he said to Waterman and, shaking Thumper's hand off his arm, went back to his seat.

Guard Simmons frowned; there was something odd here, but he couldn't put his finger on what it was, and the three men seemed to have sorted out whatever they had been discussing. There was nothing more he should do so he went back to check the tickets of the passengers who had just boarded the train.

***

It was at this moment that the private detective Hampton decided to check that his targets were still on the train. He was passing the two men in the corridor just as Thumper turned suddenly to address Waterman, his shoulder catching Mr Hampton neatly on the chin.

"Oy! Look where yer goin', yer daft sod!" Thumper snapped at him.

"But I was just passing and it was you, who—" Hampton tailed off, seeing Thumper's huge face three inches from his nose.

"It was me 'oo was wot?" Thumper's face came even closer.

"Erm – my mistake, sir." Hampton backed off and hurried away safely. He was never happy when physical danger threatened, and this situation had clearly been in that category. He decided to abandon the chase and claim danger money from the agency. He returned to his seat. He would give Harnsworth the details of the two thugs; he was sure his boss would check for any incidents reported on the train, if only to verify Hampton's story. In fact, he would talk to the guard about the incident and thus confirm what he had seen at Rugby Station. This would back his claim. Once at Crewe, he could take the next train back to Euston, claiming he had been threatened and had mislaid his regulation pistol.

***

In the corridor, Thumper looked again at Lowe, the latter sitting – quailing – in his seat.

"Wasn't we goin' ter smack 'im abaht a bit?" he hissed at Waterman in an attempted whisper heard by everyone within ten yards.

"Not here in the corridor, you half-wit, not with people watching!" Waterman's whispered response only reached Thumper's ears.

"Ho yus; yer sed in the bog, dintcher? Where I could 'ave a bit o' peace like, ter sort 'im aht proper." Thumper's agreement was at least one decibel quieter.

"Exactly, now go and sit down again, while I keep an eye on his movements. I'll call you when he needs to visit the toilet."

"An' after I've done 'im over, we can go fer a scoff? Me belly finks me froat's bin cut."

Thumper had heard that expression a few weeks back and liked it. He went back to their compartment, deciding which scoff he would need: *A mug o' tea and a large bun to kick off wiv, to ease the 'unger, like. Then a cheese sarnie – one 'o them cheeses wiv little blue bits in 'em - an' a big 'am roll wiv some 'o that mustid wot takes the roof ov yer mouf off. O yeah, an' a pint ter finish off. That'll do it till we gets a proper meal.*

Waterman shook his head again, guessing (with some accuracy) what Thumper was hoping to eat, and sighed in exasperation. *The man's only got two thoughts in his head: his fist and his stomach. What's happened to his brain? Does he even have one?*

CHAPTER 5

A Slaughter through Stafford

After leaving Rugby Station, Lady Marchant was bored. She had read her magazine twice already, and there was little of interest in it. She was pleased to note that there had been almost no mention of the minor, yet unfortunately public, *slip*, as she now described it to herself. Her initial fury at the reaction of those present at the ball, which had led to her decision to abandon London, she now considered may have been quite possibly premature. In fact, she was already reconsidering; had she been too precipitate? Would it not perhaps be possible that the slip would have been forgotten in a few months? Could she perhaps next July be able to persuade her friend Mrs Donaldson to spend a month or two in London with her ear to the ground, as it were, and then let her know whether the name of Marchant was still being bandied about with a certain disrespect, if not outright mockery? If her name had not crept into conversation within that month, then she could travel back herself for a spell in a respectable Mayfair hotel and ascertain whether it would be prudent to return on a more permanent basis. She would have to re-employ staff, of course, but her late husband had left her with sufficient funds before he had thankfully passed away. The louse had not had time to indulge himself any further with those dreadful tarts he associated with, she thought with malicious pleasure. He would have no more fun at her expense, and neither would the tarts! She could resume her rightful and well-deserved place in the capital's good society.

These and similar thoughts took her past Nuneaton and her gaze moved to the window but the fleeting glimpses of buildings or trees close to the line hardly inspired great thoughts. Her mind then began a desultory wander around her compartment. It paused at the illustrations in neat and disciplined rows above the seats, advertising holiday resorts. She thought vaguely about visiting one or two of them, before her glance landed once more on her only companion. He was busily engaged in reading a play by that disgusting man Wilde. She recalled why Wilde had spent time in prison; sex was a degrading and pointless exercise anyway, unless of course you wanted children. Then you simply had to put up with it. Why in Heaven's name did the good lord put women through such a beastly procedure? Surely He could have had a better and more dignified means of increasing the numbers of His favourite beings! But for a man to do it with another man, why that was... She couldn't think of an adequate description, and her mind paused briefly to follow along a siding. What exactly did the two men do to each other anyway? But much better not to pursue such a degrading topic; leave the foul creatures to their own loathsome habits!

She once more considered Canon Jones. *No Earthly use talking to a man like that; he reads filthy books in public! And a man of the cloth too! How did the Church allow him in? At least Bob got one thing right: he did not fool around with other men. Standards are slipping badly: look at the way those stupid people at the ball, who should have known better, made such a fuss over my little slip!*

For his part, Canon Jones had noticed the lady's glance skim around the compartment and finally rest on him. He hoped she wasn't going to start a conversation and interrupt his reading. He had felt confident that she had been discouraged by his revelation about the title and author. The play really was very good and he was enjoying it, even though he was occasionally diverted by thoughts of the young priest. The presence, however, of the evil eye across the compartment rather dampened the fantasies he hoped to entertain himself with. His earlier private amusement at the convergence of Lady Bracknell's description of Miss Prism and the presence of the gorgon sitting opposite had dissipated. The canon was a man who did not find his own company boring; he could allow his imagination full reign when he was on his own. Even when he wasn't entertained by thoughts of the young priest, or other possibilities of that ilk, his imagination provided plenty of other directions into which he could happily divert it.

Yet, like Lady Marchant, the canon also had worries. In his earlier days he had often been required to counsel the young in the diocese concerning problems which included advice regarding their romantic entanglements. He was familiar with expressions of love between the males and females which closely reflected feelings he was equally familiar with, he believed. The difference was that their feelings involved members of the opposite sex, whereas his were directed to other men. Extracts in the Bible appeared to define these as evil but if these thoughts were evil, why did God permit him to have them? Were they given to him, like the Lord's testing of the Prophet Job, to prove his faith?

He knew other men sometimes had such feelings and he suspected some women did, for other women. The Catholic Church in its wisdom insisted on celibacy for its priests and nuns, but the canon had never understood this; he was glad he was an Anglican, but even the Church of England regarded homosexuality as an illness which ought to be cured. If it was, nobody had ever found a cure, he thought. Homosexuality even occurred among animals, or so he had read, but nobody had apparently seen the need to do anything about that. But these thoughts did not help to solve his dilemma. He was constantly searching for an answer, and so far he had not found one. He contemplated briefly the 'elderly female person' opposite. No chance of help there, he concluded. He turned back to Oscar Wilde; not much help there, either. Was Lady Bracknell 'of repellent aspect' too? he wondered idly.

***

Gregory stood up, took down his case from the overhead rack, and laid out a number of items on the seat. He was the sole occupant of the compartment, so he was unconcerned at producing the pistol and knife he had brought and laying them out on the cushion. He had pulled down the compartment curtain to imply that he was sleeping. If the guard came past and opened the sliding door, Gregory could drop a shirt on the weapons to conceal them. He ascertained that the pistol was loaded but with the safety catch on, and the knife was razor-sharp. Placing the pistol back in the case and the knife in his back pocket, he sat down again, removing a flat whisky bottle from his jacket and taking a relaxing swig. He decided to go back to see that all was well with Edna so he locked his case, put it back up on the rack, and made to walk along the train.

Reaching Edna's compartment, he discovered that the couple he had seen there earlier had left. Edna was dozing quietly and there was a man sitting opposite her, whom Gregory had not noticed on his previous visit. Once he got a good look at the man, he had a shock – it was Smeddle!

This had to be considered carefully. Why on earth

would Smeddle be in the same compartment as Edna? This could not be anything but pure coincidence; Smeddle could not possibly know who the sleeping lady was, nor might he recognise Gregory in his disguise. Still, Gregory drew back just to make sure. A small worry crossed his mind as he recalled hearing that Smeddle was known as something of a ladies' man. But Gregory had seen his wife in action and was certain she could handle any situation with a would-be rake. He wondered with an internal smile how Smeddle would handle the hatpin she favoured, or the swift boot in the crotch. It might teach him to be more circumspect.

Perhaps Gregory ought to intervene and introduce them to each other; it might save an unwanted distraction. Yet Smeddle had strict instructions regarding the theft and would surely not jeopardise his reward. Nevertheless, this was a situation Gregory had not anticipated. Still, he would not interfere. He walked back thoughtfully to his own seat, but he wasn't entirely happy about this unexpected situation.

***

"Ah, slow down, Johnny, just a little," called Patrick. He had recalled an enginemen's notice indicating that just past Nuneaton a stretch of track had only yesterday been repaired, and drivers had been warned to take care over it. Although Johnny was very reliable, he might not have seen the notice because he had not expected to be driving and, in any case, such notices were for the attention of the driver, who was responsible for ensuring they were read and complied with.

"Slow down?"

"Yes, this coming stretch has just been re-laid. It was in the enginemen's notices, I've only just remembered." Patrick was apologetic. "Come down to about thirty for ten minutes."

"Won't that make us lose a bit of time into Crewe?" queried Johnny.

"Yes, but I'll take any blame. In any case, I'll take the regulator again before Lichfield, then we'll make it up."

Johnny smiled; he knew what that meant. Whenever his driver wanted to make up time, he normally did, and Johnny's arms and shoulders would bear the brunt. He eased the regulator down to slow the speed of the train as they ran over the re-laid section of track. Patrick could feel that the running was still a little rough as the track bedded itself down into the new ballast under the weight of the passing train.

On the Lichfield approaches, Patrick took over the regulator once more, commenting, "Ye did very well, Johnny. If ye drive like that on yer test, ye'll likely pass it, so ye will."

Johnny smiled to himself.

***

The slowing down of the train and the temporary roughness of the otherwise smooth run shook Edna out of her slumber and she looked through the window to see the platform and lights of Lichfield glide past as their train ran through the station. *About an hour to Crewe*, she thought. *I might make a visit to the toilet.* She still felt a little sleepy and removed her hat, putting it on her seat before she left the compartment. This, it turned out, was a very unfortunate move. Smeddle had seen his chance, and decided to follow her.

The toilet showed the sign 'vacant', so Edna opened the door and entered. When she tried to shut it, there was a surprising resistance and she turned to see what had prevented its closure. Smeddle pushed it back open then came in and shut the door, locking it behind him.

"Now, you little minx," he said, smiling and grasping her shoulders. "We can have a nice, cosy little – what shall we call it? – 'get together'?" He pulled her towards him and kissed her quickly on the mouth.

Enraged, she spat at him. "Unhand me, you filthy beast!" she shouted. "I am not that sort of woman!"

"Oh but you are; I can see it in your eyes!" He reached down to lift her dress, as she frantically searched for her hatpin. Oh god! She had left her hat on the seat! The physical strength of her attacker was far greater than her own.

Always the jeweller, as he tightened his grip on the wriggling girl Smeddle noticed with surprise the diamond in her necklace. Edna tried to ease her right leg back for a vigorous swing to hit him between the legs, but he had her held firmly up against a wall and she couldn't move her leg back at all. She tried to knee him but his leg was firmly against her thigh, too close for the blow to have any effect. She tore off her glove and furiously raked her fingernails across his face, causing deep scratches.

Smeddle felt the warm blood began to flow down his cheek. "You bitch!" he snapped. He let go of her dress and grabbed her round the neck. "I'll quieten you down!" he snarled grimly and began to throttle her. He knew she had badly scratched his face. This would be difficult to explain to his wife; and what would his customers in the shop say about it?

Edna tried to loosen his hands and shout, but his grip was far too tight and she could only gasp softly as she weakened and her vision began to blur.

The door rattled as someone tried to enter, then ceased as the person saw the 'engaged' sign. Smeddle held rigidly onto Edna's neck in case she attempted to call for help, until he could hear the footsteps walking away. Finally, he relaxed his hold round her throat and Edna slumped to the floor.

Smeddle stared, horrified by what he had done. He had loosened his grip on her neck much too late for the young lady, whose eyes were beginning to lose their focus.

Smeddle opened the door and glanced out to see whether anyone was in the corridor. There was nobody there, so if he was quick there would be no one to see what he had done. But he had an afterthought, and bent to undo the necklace he had admired before leaving Edna lying on the floor with the toilet door wide open.

Through the grimy window, she vaguely noticed a signboard, 'Stafford', as the train passed through the station. It was the last thing she saw as she took her final breath and her sight faded for the last time.

Hurrying back to his seat, Smeddle sat down, breathing heavily. What the hell had he done? He straightened his cravat, wiped the blood from his face, and wondered what he should do now. No-one had seen him, and there was nothing to link him to the woman on the toilet floor, although the guard might recall that they had been in the same compartment. Even so, why should he accuse him of attacking her?

If asked, he would explain that the lady had left the compartment, presumably to go to the toilet. She had taken a long time and he had thought nothing of it; he himself was a married man and knew that ladies sometimes took far longer than men in a toilet, especially if there were a mirror available to primp in. He had decided to stay and keep an eye on her luggage so that nobody could steal it in her absence. These thoughts, he believed, were totally reasonable and convincing. There was no evidence to link him with anything untoward.

He would have to staunch any flow of blood on his face, of course. A handkerchief would take care of that; it would have to be discarded out of the window afterwards, naturally; he couldn't allow anyone to find it on his person. He would locate a different toilet, clean his face up, and then return. If asked why he didn't go to the toilet in his own coach, why then he would reply it was apparently occupied. The attacker could be anybody else in the train.

No, he was in the clear. Now he would concentrate his mind on what Gregory required of him.

In the meantime, he took Edna's necklace out of his pocket to examine it more closely. It was a quality item and much nicer than he had expected of the little tart. It even looked more like one of the items than his paste copy based on the one which Gregory had described, and would be better as a replacement. The item he had obtained wasn't really close enough to the original to be convincing. Well, that was at least one good thing that had come from the problem in the toilet. He added it to the other items he had acquired for the exchange.

***

Guard Simmons had checked all the tickets of the few passengers who had boarded the train at Rugby and was walking back to his van at the rear of the train. So far, it had been a peaceful run, apart from that odd incident at Rugby, with fewer passengers than he would normally expect. He checked his watch as they ran through Stafford. They had slowed a little where the track had recently been re-laid. He at first thought that Patrick may have forgotten the speed restriction; he had left it rather late, but the train had slowed down suddenly. Herbert grinned as he thought of Patrick's language as he remembered just in time. Driver O'Leary didn't like to be caught in error.

But then... what was this? A toilet door left open? Good heavens, some passengers were so careless! Herbert hurried to shut the door and was shocked to find a lady lying motionless on the toilet floor. Had she fainted? He leaned in to help her up, but she was totally limp. He saw that her eyes were wide open, apparently in shock. Feeling for a pulse, he realised he could not establish one. She was dead! Guard Simmons looked more carefully and observed angry red marks on the lady's neck. She had been throttled! He checked his watch; they would be stopping in Crewe in less than twenty minutes, and he could call for urgent assistance there.

Quickly, he locked the toilet door to ensure that nobody could interfere with the body, in what was clearly the scene of a murder. The police would need to search for evidence of precisely what had happened here. He sighed. Gone was the peaceful run. An ambulance would have to be called and the police would be asking questions, which would hold up the train. There would be a lengthy report to write, and there would be no end of official enquiries for him to deal with. The train would be held up and the sleeping-car attendants would be required to show the police into all berths for questions.

He returned to his van, took out a sheet of paper, and quickly began to write down anything that might have a bearing on the matter. The police would want to ask him all sorts of questions, and it would be best to have some answers ready, even though he had no idea of who might be involved. Wait! Wasn't she the pretty woman in the compartment with an elderly couple and a middle-aged gent? The couple had left the train at Rugby, and he was sure the lady had still been in the compartment afterwards. The other man had still been there too. He might know something helpful. On the other hand, he might just say that she left to presumably visit the toilet and didn't return. Well, that would be for the coppers to sort out.

Simmons checked his watch a third time: only seventeen minutes to Crewe. They would arrive on time, and he could go off duty after explaining to the police everything that he could recall. Patrick and young Winslowe would not be detained long, either; they could not add anything of value to the investigation as there was no possible human connection between the locomotive and the rest of the train. The replacement guard and enginemen on the Crewe to Holyhead shift would have to handle the situation and explain the late arrival in Holyhead, because the train would be very late, Simmons had little doubt about that. How the police might deal with the situation, he had no idea, but thankfully that was not his problem.

CHAPTER 6

A Cut Thread at Crewe

Driver O'Leary, catching sight of the first signals indicating the approach to Crewe, lowered the regulator gently to slow the speed of the train. The approach down Madeley Bank had assisted late drivers many times to make up time before their arrival, but Patrick O'Leary knew there were several sets of points to negotiate before arriving in the main down platform. Over twenty years later, this set of points was to almost derail a record-breaking streamlined locomotive with its train, as its driver failed to slow down sufficiently to negotiate them safely. But Patrick's care allowed the Irish Mail to arrive and stop gently and without fuss, as passengers moved forward to the doors to leave the train as it pulled in at the main up platform. Here too were a few passengers on the platform and porters moving to judge where the doors would be when the train finally stopped.

Guard Herbert Simmons, hanging out of his door as the train slowed, called out urgently to station staff for railway police to attend to train. Within minutes the police had arrived and, after a brief conversation, called for reinforcements which also arrived with alacrity. Passengers attempting to board were held up while police constables tried to hold those leaving the train; they were required for questioning. Two police inspectors and a detective sergeant arrived with detective constables; one inspector and the DS were shown into the toilet, where Edna Clayton's corpse was carefully examined. The inspector noted details of the crime scene and then directed his constables to move through the train, with Guard Simmons questioning the passengers. Those in the sleeping cars showed their irritation at being disturbed in their slumber but most were co-operative as soon as they understood the reason. Those who were not were threatened with being taken from the train for more detailed questioning at the local police station; this produced a rapid change of attitude.

It was obvious that the Mail was going to be held up for more than its timetabled four minutes, and it was considerably longer before the train was cleared once more for departure. The police had been able to discover very little of value and the police sergeant decided to stay on the train to its destination, accompanied by two police constable. They would see whether any more helpful evidence might turn up.

***

At first, unaware of any unusual activity, Patrick gathered his lunch box and Johnny finished his sweeping of the cab floor; he did not like to leave a dirty cab for his replacement fireman. But before the new crew could board the cab, a railway official inspector climbed aboard.

"Driver O'Leary and Fireman Winslowe, there has been a change of duty. Instead of returning to Euston, you and your fireman are to continue your shift to Holyhead with this engine. There you will stay overnight, returning tomorrow with a Euston express still to be determined. After that, you get a day's break."

Patrick was surprised. "Why's that, sir?"

"It's partly for your own benefit, Driver O'Leary. I am informed that there's a gentleman from the Great Southern and Western Railway of Ireland waiting in Holyhead to talk to you with regard to your application for a transfer. The North-Western regrets losing you but appreciates the problem you have, and is willing to assist you in this. It was also felt that the views of your regular fireman might conceivably be an advantage in any interview."

Speechless, Patrick shook his head, before he found words. "That's very generous, sir. I don't know what to say!" Then he looked at his fireman. "Alright with you, Johnny?"

"Of course, Mr O'Leary. I'll be glad to help if I can."

"Now," continued the inspector, "I mentioned that this change of duty was partly a favour to you, but there is another reason: we want to know what your engine is capable of if pushed, Driver. Can you take her on to Holyhead, do you think?"

Patrick glanced at the tender. "We might need to coal her again, sir, but aside from that we should be fine. I know there are water troughs outside Prestatyn."

"That would save time, I'll warn Chester to be ready to coal you. But–" he looked out of the cab – "there seems to be some trouble along the platform. I don't know why the police are there. You might be waiting a while yet. I'll go and see what's up." He climbed down and walked along to where the police were active.

Judging from the police activity, there was going to be a longer wait, so Patrick sent Johnny to the refreshment room to bring mugs of tea and a couple of sandwiches to tide them along as far as Holyhead. It wasn't really enough for two hungry men, but they were short of time. The police had interviewed the few disembarking passengers and had removed the body of Edna Clayton, as well as checked the toilet for any evidence.

The new guard, Henry Adams, came to inform them of what had happened.

"A murder?" Patrick was astounded. "On our train? I've had a few incidents in me life in the cab, but nivver a murder before on me train!"

The police detective sergeant climbed into the cab to ask his questions, but it was obvious that the enginemen could not help, and he returned with the guard to the train.

***

Lowe was gazing with close interest out of the window. What was this? Coppers everywhere! How could he use them to escape from the clutches of the two thugs who were after him? As a policeman walked past in the corridor, Lowe stood up abruptly, grabbed his case from the luggage rack, and jumped from the train. As he hurried away, a nearby constable stopped him. "Sorry, sir. Nobody's allowed out just yet."

"But I have to leave the train here," Lowe protested.

"All passengers will be allowed to leave, sir, when our enquiries are complete," the constable assured him. "Just wait here for a few minutes."

"But I have to catch another train!"

"All trains in Crewe are stopped until we are ready, sir," the constable said firmly.

Watching carefully were Jeff Waterman and Thumper Dawson. Waterman had stepped nearer to Lowe's compartment, with a view to discouraging any sudden exit but his efforts had been frustrated. He held his hand firmly on Thumper's chest to prevent the man from rushing forward. "Wait, you daft bugger!" he hissed. "There's coppers about!"

Thumper caught sight of the police and stopped suddenly. "Wot do they want?" he asked hoarsely. "We ain't done nuthin'." Thumper's reaction on seeing police was instant and instinctive, brought on by long and frequent need.

"No, but you were about to."

"I woulda' stopped, when I seed 'em."

"You might have, but then you might not have."

"Fight in front o' coppers? I'm not bloody silly!" replied Thumper angrily. "Don't keep callin' me stoopid!"

"You'd be in clink long ago if I hadn't stopped you from doing something stupid." Waterman was getting tired of his complaining and unreliable mate.

Thumper lifted his fist and waved it in front of Waterman's nose. "Yer seen me fist workin' often enough. Yer want to see 'ow it 'urts?"

"Now you're being stupid again."

Thumper's fist swung back to take a swing at his partner, but his arm was grabbed firmly from behind. The constable who had stopped Lowe had been distracted by the apparent altercation and had hold of Thumper's arm, and was studying the fist.

"That looks very like an attack, sir; and you appear to be about to inflict a spot of GBH on another man. That's illegal, sir." The constable smiled as he reached for a set of handcuffs.

"Er – no, Constable." Waterman broke in quickly, putting his hands up in protest. "We were just having a little fun."

"Didn't look like fun to me, sir," replied the constable, but he replaced his handcuffs.

While all this was going on, Lowe had taken his chance, glanced around and dropped to the track between two coaches. He then walked across the central tracks to the opposite platform and climbed up. Nonchalantly, he headed towards the nearest exit, but found it blocked by two more policemen. He turned quickly and started to walk back, but it was too late; he had been noticed and one of the constables hurried over to him.

"Just one moment, sir. I need to ask you a few questions."

Lowe turned and said, "Sorry, Constable. Did you want something?"

"Yes, sir. My inspector would like to interview any passenger wishing to leave the station. Which train did you just come from?"

Fast thinking was not Lowe's forte. "Oh, um – a Manchester train."

"And where were you planning to go?"

"Oh, er – Chester." It was the first place he thought of.

"The constable pointed over the track to the Mail. "That train is next stop Chester. Why were you going to the exit?"

"I must have been misinformed. Thank you for the information. I'll head for that train straightaway."

"The footbridge is over there, sir." The policeman pointed to the bridge over the tracks. As Lowe walked off, the constable muttered to his mate, "Keep an eye on 'im, Jack; I don't believe a bloody word 'e says. Follow 'im an' make sure 'e's spoken to by the sergeant."

His mate nodded and began to follow.

In the meantime, Waterman had been able to cool Thumper down, and the police had left them. Waterman noticed that Lowe had vanished. "Look there!" he said to Thumper. "While you were messing me and the copper around, that Lowe bloke has buggered off. We have to find the little sod!"

***

In their compartment, a policeman had arrived to ask questions of James and Harriet. At first, Harriet assumed that the police were looking for them, and was wondering how they could deflect any suspicion about their tickets to Gretna. Then she remembered that they were on the Irish Mail, which she knew did not go north from Crewe.

"Your destination, miss?" the constable asked.

"Chester, Officer," replied Harriet, nudging James gently. "I have an aunt in Chester."

Chester? wondered James. *Does she have an aunt in Chester? Is that in Scotland? Perhaps we could stay with this aunt and save money.*

"And you, sir?" asked the constable, looking at James. "Er, yes, Chester. We're together."

"Thank you, sir. And you, sir?" he asked of the man sitting next to James.

"Holyhead and then Ireland," the man replied.

After questioning the remaining passengers, the constable nodded to them and left, sliding the door shut. Harriet closed her eyes and visibly relaxed.

They ought to have changed trains here in Crewe, but the arrival and questions of the constable had distracted them, and both remained in their seats after the train left. Harriet was relieved that the nice policeman had not asked to see their tickets; that would have made him instantly suspicious.

"You alright, my love?" asked James, leaning over to his bride-to-be solicitously.

"Yes, dear, just a little tired."

James leaned back and smiled. He enjoyed being called 'dear'. It sounded so right! Harriet closed her eyes in feigned sleep. Then it occurred to James they ought to have changed here; weren't they supposed to change at Crewe? But there were simply too many police about; they couldn't possibly change trains now and risk more questions. Why on earth had the police come to question the passengers on the train? Did this sort of thing always happen on train journeys, or was it just a procedure at Crewe? What was the point of it anyway? James was not a man used to dealing with anything other than his daily run-of-the mill situations and he was not equipped with the mental capacity for such complexities.

***

On the opposite platform, Lowe had escaped the frying pan and now had to deal with the fire. He had realised that he was being followed and decided to try and shake off the copper who was after him. He accelerated his walk slightly, hurried round the corner of the refreshment room, opened the door and pulled to shut it as he passed. He ran further towards the footbridge and hid behind a pile of crates. The constable hurried round the corner, saw the refreshment room door swinging shut, and went in. There were very few people in room as it was past midnight, and the room would shut once the Irish Mail had left. By the time the constable realised he had been misled, there was no sign of Lowe, who had slipped over the bridge and come down to see the passengers waiting to board the train he had left a few minutes earlier. He turned quickly and walked further along the footbridge to another platform and descended just in time to meet another figure, waiting with a smile on his face.

"Nice ter meet yer agen, Mr Lowe," said Thumper. "I was 'opin' ter see yer so we could finish our little bisness, wot was so rudely 'alted by them coppers." He dug into his pocket, pulled out the knuckleduster, and flexed his hands; he slipped his instrument onto his fist while Lowe watched in horrified fascination.

"I've, er – I've got some c-cash you can have, if you l-leave me alone," he stuttered in desperation, hauling out two ten-pound notes.

"'Ave yer now?" Thumper paused; he was interested in pound notes. He didn't often see any; Jeff always paid him only in coins, and never enough of them. He wondered if the bloke had any more notes; he would see. He hit Lowe very hard and fast in the stomach.

Lowe gasped in agony; he had never felt such pain

before in his life. He bent over to vomit and Thumper lifted his knee and hit Lowe with it in the face as he folded over. Lowe collapsed on the floor of the footbridge. Thumper went through his pockets, found a dozen more pound notes, and transferred their ownership to L. Dawson Esq.

Pleased, he stamped carefully on Lowe's leg and, hearing the crack of a broken bone, left feeling vindicated that he had fulfilled his duty. He liked to give full satisfaction for any job he had been tasked to complete.

"Change at Crewe inter a hambulance," he grinned as he walked back to report to Waterman. He might forget to tell Jeff about the notes. Serve the bugger right for always calling him stupid.

Then, in an unusual moment of sympathy, he waited behind a corner until he saw a police constable catch sight of Lowe's body lying further along the footbridge, and shout to two colleagues. They hurried to Lowe and, discovering his injuries, two of them picked him up gently, while the third ran back to call for an ambulance. Thumper smiled. *Inter horspittle yer go, mate, 'an we'll 'ave fifty nicker each, me an' Jeff by nex' week! Five more notes to add ter the ones I found in Lowe's pocket!* he thought with pleasure as he walked back, polishing a fleck of blood which had somehow got on to his favourite knuckleduster.

"Oi! One moment, matey."

"Wot?" Thumper stopped and stared at the copper who was interrupting his thoughts.

"Nice to see a perfessional lookin' after 'is tools," remarked the policeman, staring at the knuckleduster with interest.

"Yeah, just got a spot o' blood on it," explained Thumper, continuing with his polishing.

"Off some bloke's chin, p'raps?"

"Yeah, belted 'im good'n proper an' —" Thumper suddenly realised who he was chatting to. "Er– wot bloke?"

"Where'd you leave 'im?" asked the policeman quickly.

"'E's on the footbri—" Thumper stopped.

"What's that on your back?" asked the policeman.

Thumper turned to show his back, "Nuthin'."

"Yes, just 'ere," said the policeman, touching Thumper's back.

Thumper felt round with his hands, "There's nuthin' there!"

"There is now," said the policeman, clapping handcuffs on Thumper's wrists. He didn't want any resistance from a professional thug who had a knuckleduster and presumably knew how to use it. He removed the knuckleduster from Thumper's hand and pocketed it; that would be handy as evidence.

"We need you to answer some questions about a dead lady found in the toilet of a train," said the policeman conversationally as he marched Thumper to his inspector.

Dead molly? thought Thumper in fright. *We 'aven't topped a molly! Orlright, I done a bloke over but surely they couldn't put a murder dahn ter me!*

Although he'd bashed plenty of people, he'd never actually topped anyone. *An' that bloke wot I done over; they know 'e ain't dead.*

Thumper was marched along the platform past Waterman, who was standing in the train watching him with cold eyes. But as Thumper glared up in an appeal for assistance, Waterman made no move to climb down and explain anything.

Why the 'ell did Jeff not come aht and tell them coppers that we 'ad nothing ter do wiv any toppin'? Thumper thought. *Jeff's supposed to be looking after me! Come on yer sod, come dahn outta that train an' say somefing!*

***

Gregory was aware that the stop in Crewe could be longer than usual because quite a lot of luggage needed to be transferred from trains from Glasgow, Manchester or Liverpool to the mail train for Ireland. His planned theft was in his mind, and he was distracted by the entrance into his compartment of some damn fool of a policeman who had ridiculous questions about a corpse in a toilet. What would he know about a corpse in a toilet?

Gregory decided to wait until the train started again before going to chat with Edna. He determined to carry out the theft between Chester and Holyhead and would need to have Smeddle with him to effect the transfer of the items out of Sir Alexander's case to be replaced with whatever Smeddle had brought with him.

He hoped Smeddle had found similar but cheaper items for the transfer; they might pass a cursory inspection but wouldn't fool a jeweller for a moment. Yet the chances of Sir Alexander having a pet jeweller on the train were very small. However, mused Gregory grimly, if Smeddle had botched anything, he would bitterly regret it. Smeddle would know that; if not, he would discover his error very swiftly indeed.

While he was engaged in these ruminations, he took little notice of what was happening on the platform. As a consequence, he did not see the care with which a body was brought out of a coach and loaded onto a stretcher. It was wheeled away on a station trolley guarded by three medical orderlies and two police constables as it was taken up the stairway to the station entrance to await an ambulance which had already been called for.

He glanced out of the window. Whatever had interested the police had apparently now been sorted out; passengers were moving about normally. And there was the guard standing on the platform with his green flag, ready to signal the belated departure. The flag was waved, a whistle from the engine sounded, and the train began to move gently away on its interrupted journey to Holyhead.

Now, thought Gregory, his attention moving instantly to the planned theft, *Only Chester still to come and after that I will call on Smeddle and we will discuss exactly when to conduct our little exchange of my noble friend's jewels.*

CHAPTER 7

Chivalry in Chester

With all these policemen running about and asking inane questions of simple, law-abiding passengers, Lady Marchant was highly indignant. This was Crewe, and she had to change trains here. Her ticket was clearly marked for Manchester and the police had no right whatsoever to prevent her from leaving the train! What was wrong with them? Why all this foolishness? If she were forced to travel to Holyhead against her wishes, she would demand to see the Chief Constable of Wales, or whoever was in charge. Nobody was going to take advantage of this elderly lady; they would discover that she was not one of the country's lower orders; she was the wife of the late, distinguished Sir Robert Marchant!

Her husband's distinction was a sudden invention which would have vastly amused him, had he been alive to learn about it.

Furthermore, her thoughts continued, she wanted to change her train to be away from this dreadful canon, with his dreadful book. It was a disgrace that the Anglican Church should allow someone of that nature to become a person of authority. The late dear King Edward had limited his reputedly improper interests at least to ladies, she thought fondly, regretting for a brief moment that she herself had not received any invitation from him to a private visit. Perhaps she ought somehow to let King George know what his Church was up to. The new king was thought to be a highly respectable man, and would not tolerate such appalling laxity. Wasn't he head of the Church of England, anyway?

When a policeman entered their compartment to make risible enquiries about a dead female in a toilet, she told him that she refused to answer such unbelievable impertinence. Did he imagine she was a person capable of such absurdity? She was strongly tempted to recommend him to examine the canon. Now there was a man far more likely to engage in depravity; just look at the book he was reading! *And hiding the title, too,* she added mentally. Although, and here she had to be honest with herself, if the dead person were a lady, then the canon would seem to be an unlikely candidate for such a crime. She so angered herself with these thoughts that she failed to notice that the whistle had been blown and the train had begun to move in the direction of Holyhead.

The train accelerated past the Crewe North engine sheds and was rumbling past the North Western's vast workshops on the right before Lady Marchant belatedly grasped that she had missed leaving the train at Crewe. She was now committed to the North Wales line. Why on earth had a porter not come and assisted her with her luggage? Surely that's what they were there for. She would write an irate letter to the railway company, demanding instant compensation and an assurance that all Crewe porters would be heavily fined.

Shortly after departure, the door slid open and Guard Adams looked in. "Did you board the train at Crewe, Madam - or you, sir?"

This was Lady D's chance. She began her attack. "No, young man, I did not. And I wish you to explain why I was not permitted to leave this train at Crewe. I have a ticket to Manchester, and I needed to change trains at Crewe, but instead of calling for a porter, I was asked some nonsensical questions about a dead body in a toilet. How ridiculous. The behaviour of the railway staff has been utterly disgraceful, and I shall want a full explanation!"

Henry Adams was unperturbed. "I regret to inform you, madam, that a serious crime has been committed on this train and a lady's corpse has been found. The holdup was at the request of the Crewe police, and we were naturally obliged to co-operate. It is unfortunate that you have been inconvenienced but, as I am sure you will appreciate, the matter has been rather worse for the young lady concerned. I suggest that you change trains in Chester in about–" he took out his watch and glanced at it – "twenty-two minutes. You will be able to catch a train direct to Manchester from there." A quick glance at the canon's ticket and a muttered "Thank you, sir," and he slid the door shut firmly, denying her any suitable response, which left her fuming.

"Really! The insolence of railway staff is beyond belief!" she spoke with feeling to the compartment.

Canon Jones sighed theatrically. "Yes, madam," he agreed reluctantly, but what was for him beyond belief was that he was to be lumbered with the woman for another twenty minutes. Personally, he was deeply impressed by the way that the guard had handled the lady so masterfully; the episode had shone like a small flame of delight in the darkness. Nevertheless, Christian charity suggested that he should offer to assist the lady with her luggage at the next stop, if only to ensure that she left the train.

***

"Rhyl to Conway, Johnny, and she's yours again," remarked Patrick to his fireman. "Let's see how you deal with a problem." This was spoken with a grin.

"Problem, Mr O'Leary? What problem? Not one of your tricks?"

Driver O'Leary was known throughout Camden Shed as a man with a penchant for practical jokes. Patrick didn't often try them on Johnny because he had discovered that his fireman was too smart to be caught often and, if he were, Patrick could expect a disconcerting retaliation.

"No, nothing like that. I wouldn't do that to you

when you're driving. No, the stop in Chester might be longer if we have to detach and pick up some coal before going on. What we've still got in the tender won't get us to Holyhead."

"Why don't they change engines, or give us a pilot?"

"I expect they want to see whether a Claughton can manage a longer run."

"Well, thank you anyway. I'd enjoy another stint on the regulator. The sheer power in this engine is exhilarating."

Patrick nodded while looking through the spectacle plate, checking for the next set of signals to see that all was clear through the little station of Beeston Castle. The village itself had really been too small to warrant a station but for many years a local aristocrat, who owned the land the LNWR needed for its route, had insisted on them building a station there as a condition for his agreement. He had also insisted that all trains must stop there. It had taken years of legal work before the company could run its expresses through without stopping. Even stopping trains had few passengers using the station, and quite frequently none at all.

There was no point in opening the locomotive up to increase speed with the stop at Chester less than fifteen minutes distant. Passengers to Ireland from the GWR south of Chester could be expected to join the train here, so the stop was an important one.

They were half an hour late in Chester, and an inspector on the platform called up to Patrick. "Take your engine to the GWR shed, Driver, and fill up on coal there. The Great Western has agreed to sell us their coal to get you away faster." The GWR engine shed was only fifty yards away, whereas the LNWR shed was half a mile back towards Crewe.

"Nip out and uncouple her, Johnny," Patrick told his fireman. "I'll be back in a jiffy." He waited until he heard the call from the track that the uncoupling was complete then he eased his engine away to the GWR shed to coal up. He was back again within fifteen minutes and Johnny coupled up once more.

***

Near the rear of the train, Gregory finally got up from his seat and went along to the luggage van to see ex-Sergeant Thorpe. Gregory knew that he had been unusually fortunate in picking up Thorpe; that careless call of DCI Brown when Gregory had been to see him had paid off handsomely. According to the sergeant, he had been forced to retire because valuable items, confiscated during local crimes, had tended to vanish from the evidence bag when he was on duty. Nothing could be proved, but the Detective Chief Inspector had been certain that Thorpe was responsible. Of course, all this was nonsense, claimed the ex-sergeant. Gregory knew that was a lie but was unconcerned; such ex-coppers with a deep resentment for the police had very useful knowledge and experience.

The train guard was away, checking passengers' tickets. Gregory tapped on the window of the luggage van and Thorpe got up and opened the door to let him in. He showed Gregory the little lock-pick he had brought. "Very handy, this, Mr Gregory."

"All well, Thorpe?"

"Yes, Mr Gregory. There's been no problem so far. When do you intend to make the exchange?"

"When is the train guard likely to have some free time?"

"Guard Adams usually takes a short fifteen-minute break, he told me, between Rhyl and Llandudno Junction, when he eats his sandwiches and reads a paper."

"And when will that be?"

"We're running a little behind time so I am not certain, but at a guess I would say in about an hour's time."

"I'll return with my colleague then. We should be able to make the exchange in five minutes easily."

"Very good, Mr Gregory. I'll be ready for you, and we'll unlock the case."

Gregory nodded again and left the van to return to his seat.

***

As the train had begun to slow down to stop in Chester, Canon Jones stood up and reached for Lady Marchant's case.

"What on earth are you doing, sir?" demanded the astonished lady.

"I'm so sorry, madam. I assumed you were

planning to leave the train in Chester. I merely wanted to assist you with your luggage. You may find it difficult to find a porter at this time of night."

Lady Marchant had spoken with vigour but modified her tone quickly. After all, the man had only been trying to help.

"Oh, of course. I do beg your pardon. Well in that case, thank you."

"Not at all. But you might need to stand near the door because the train might not stop for long."

"Yes, you are right." She found it uneasy being civil to a man of whom she heartily disapproved, but moved willingly into the corridor. The man was perfectly correct, she discovered. There were very few passengers in the train or on the platform, apart from a young couple many yards away. The canon came down to the platform with her case and placed it next to her while she searched for a porter.

He returned to his seat with a heartfelt smile on his face as the train began to move away gently once more. "Thank the Lord for that!" he murmured piously.

***

Lady M stared around the empty platform. There was nobody about; even that young couple had disappeared. Where were the porters to help her? Where was the Manchester train? Manchester was such an important place, it had to be from an important platform. That would naturally be a platform with a first or second number. She searched for Platform One, found it some distance away, and walked there, carrying her case, but the platform was very short. *This cannot be the right platform*, she thought. *Manchester deserves a longer platform than this.* The adjacent Platform Two was far longer. *This will be it*, she thought, and she sat on a nearby bench to wait for the next train, and dozed off.

She woke up four hours later to find the platform full of people of a lower class. Workers on their way to Manchester, she concluded. When she boarded, struggling with her case, she was horrified to discover that the train had no first-class compartments. She had to sit with some common people and then, once in the train, she realised that she needed a lavatory. She got up to open the door to the corridor but discovered to her shock that there was none; the door opened to the track, and the train was leaving. She sat down again, dazed; what in Heaven's name was this train? She simply sat there until she left the train at the first stop seven minutes later. The station sign read 'Upton-by-Chester' and had a short wooden platform with a small office on the opposite track. After waiting in vain for a porter, she stumbled across the tracks with her case and walked to the little office, which had a toilet next door. She entered in great relief until she saw that the toilet was very cramped, there was no paper or washing facility, and the place had apparently been omitted from the cleaning roster for some months.

The official in the tiny ticket office next door was

surprised to see Lady Marchant, but was immediately helpful and took up his telephone to speak to someone in Authority. It was another hour before she could catch the next uncomfortable train back to Chester's General Station and she could find a Manchester-bound train from there.

"Chorlton, madam?" asked an elderly porter. "To be honest, your best bet is to get a cab to Chester's Northgate Station and catch a Cheshire Lines train to Manchester Central. That train will let you off at Stretford. A cab there will get you home in fifteen minutes. If you take one of our trains, you'd go to Manchester Exchange and then you'd need to get a cab to Central Station and get to Chorlton from there. That'd take a lot longer."

Finally, thought Lady Marchant, *a helpful railway official!*

"Thank you so much, my man." She gave him a half-sovereign in her relief.

The porter tipped his cap respectfully and stared in disbelief at the coin in his hand. "'Alf a sov!" he muttered in shock, as she left him. "Bess won't believe this!"

***

Shortly before arriving at Chester, Guard Adams reached the compartment containing James and Harriet, both of whom had dozed off. He smiled as he saw the young couple resting together with contented expressions on their faces; he recognised their mutual feelings because he had been married himself only three months earlier. He was reluctant to wake them, but he had to do his job.

"Excuse me, sir and madam. I need to see your tickets." He spoke loudly and waited for them to surface.

"Wha-? Tickets? What tickets?" James woke first.

"Your ticket, sir."

"Ah, yes. Tickets." James fumbled around, searching his pocket.

"Blast! Where is it?" he muttered.

Harriet woke up at his voice. "Language, dear, language!"

The chide was gentle but unmistakable. Language? What language? Was 'Blast' bad language? It had been common in the Sixth Form at Ridley. Well at least, there was that 'dear' again.

"The guard wants our tickets," he explained.

"Tickets? Yes, of course," she replied, then spoke to the guard. "I'm afraid there was a fuss at Crewe and in the confusion, we forgot to leave the train to change for another to Scotland. What would be our best plan?"

"Scotland, madam? That's not a major problem. You need to change at Chester, the next stop in a few minutes. There you can take a Manchester train and change in Warrington, where you can catch a connection to Carlisle. From Carlisle, take another on to Scotland. You won't need to purchase another ticket, except from Chester to Warrington. Your tickets are valid from Warrington to Scotland, and," he added with a smile, "I won't charge you for your trip from Crewe to Chester."

"That's very kind of you," replied Harriet, relieved that they would soon be back on track. The guard leaned down towards her and whispered, "Give my regards to the blacksmith!"

After checking the tickets of the other passengers, he left, grinning.

"Gretna!" he laughed quietly in the corridor. "I hope they get there before anyone stops them."

"What did he whisper to you, Harriet? Did he say something about a blacksmith?" asked James curiously. He wasn't at all happy at a strange man whispering to his intended; even a man they would never see again. What the hell did he mean, talking about a blacksmith? A passenger sitting opposite put his hand in front of his mouth as he coughed and stared pointedly out of the window. James noticed the man's shoulders shaking for some reason.

Harriet chuckled. "Nothing important, dear. Er – we must get ready to leave the train in a few minutes." She loved James dearly, but she had long recognised and accepted his limited mental acuity.

"Oh, er – yes; suitcases," said James, standing up to take their cases from the luggage rack in preparation to leave the train as it gradually drew to a standstill. Once they were standing on the platform he asked, "Are we going to see your aunt in Chester now?" He was looking forward to meeting this aunt who, from the way Harriet talked, seemed to be on their side.

"Oh dear," sighed Harriet. "Darling, you know I love you and want to marry you, but you must learn to use your brain sometimes. I have no aunt, neither here in Chester nor in Scotland."

"But you said—"

"Yes, but I was lying to get us out of trouble!"

"Aren't we out of trouble? That guard said—"

"James, once we are in Gretna Green and married, we will be out of trouble. Until then, anyone can stop us, so we will need to take care that nobody does."

"Well, what do we do now?" James looked around the huge, dark station. In the early hours of the morning, there was nobody around.

As they were standing there, an office door opened not far away and a man came out, saw them and came over.

"You two young people look a bit lost," he said. "Can I help you?"

Harriet said, "Thank you, yes. Can you sell us a ticket to Warrington?"

"A ticket?" The man shook his head. "No, I'm sorry," he replied regretfully. "I'm only a timetable clerk on night duty. I'm not even a North-Western man: I work for the Great Western. The ticket office won't be manned now, but the guard on the train will sell you a ticket. Where d'you need to go?" Harriet told him and he pulled out a watch.

"There's an express for Manchester in about an hour. Expresses for Manchester stop at Warrington. They usually depart from Platform Ten over the footbridge. Could you use a cup of tea? I'm having my tea break. The refreshment rooms are shut but there is a little railwaymen's canteen open. I'm sure they will offer you something. Come with me." He led them away along a poorly lit part of the station to a small door with a lamp over it. Inside were a few benches and a bored girl serving at the counter. They had a snack and the clerk took them back and showed them the footbridge to Platform Ten.

They waited until an express came then climbed in and sat down in an empty compartment until a guard came past.

"Two third-class singles to Warrington? Certainly, sir."

James handed over the money to the guard, who clipped them and handed them back. "Warrington in half an hour, sir and madam."

"Don't for heaven's sake fall asleep, James," remarked Harriet. "We don't want to miss our connection to Scotland."

James nodded fondly at Harriet. *How lucky I am,* he thought. *My bride is both beautiful and intelligent.*

He was right on both counts.

CHAPTER 8

Booty near Bangor

After leaving Chester, most of the 200-odd passengers on the train were fast asleep. This included the dozen or so who had boarded there. Gregory decided to go along to have a quiet chat with Edna and see that all was well with her and Smeddle. He had concluded that it was actually quite convenient that both of them were together because he would only need to discuss the detail of the exchange of jewellery once without having to repeat himself. But when he arrived at her compartment, Edna was not there. Nor was her case. Only Smeddle sat there, checking an item of jewellery.

"Where's the young lady who was sitting in this compartment, Smeddle?"

The jeweller looked up, his eyes widening. How did this man know his name? He looked carefully before replying; there was something about those eyes – good god, it was Gregory!

"I'm so sorry, Mr Gregory, I didn't recognise you at first. The young lady got out at Crewe, I think."

"You think? Don't you know?"

"Just before Crewe she went out with her case, I imagine to the toilet. She didn't return so I supposed she had left the train." Smeddle omitted to say that the police had been in and had taken her luggage.

"Hmm." Gregory decided not to mention that the girl was his wife. Where could she be? Why the hell would she get out in Crewe? He walked slowly back along the train to the luggage van to speak to Thorpe again. Edna, unlike Smeddle, was not essential to the jewellery exchange. Well, she would have to wait until he returned to London, then he would find out why she had decided to leave the train at Crewe without informing him. She had better have a very good explanation for not being in her seat when he came looking!

Thorpe was chewing a sandwich when Gregory came in. "So soon, Mr Gregory?" he asked as he saw him. "I thought you were aiming to wait until we passed Rhyl."

"Yes, I haven't changed my mind. I just wondered why we waited so long in Crewe."

"Yes, well that had me worried for a few minutes," Thorpe admitted. "I thought we had been rumbled. The police were everywhere, asking questions."

"Yes, they even asked me a couple of questions about a body in the train toilet, of all things!"

"I had the same questions asked of me. I was

getting very unhappy, I can tell you. But I spoke to the young guard later. He told me there had been a fight or something on the train."

"A fight?"

"Yes, someone was left badly hurt in a toilet, thought to be somewhere near Stafford, he said."

"Who was hurt?"

"Couldn't tell you that, guv'nor. The train guard didn't know, and the coppers weren't telling. But he thought they arrested a big bloke on the platform, perhaps there'd been a punch-up in the toilet and the big bloke had won and tried to scarper."

Gregory's first thought was that seemed quite possible. He had heard of a major quarrel between two gangs in South London, over which controlled the Wimbledon area. But that didn't explain his missing wife. Could these two things be linked?

An idea struck him: could Smeddle have tried something on with Edna? Gregory had seen her in action with a hatpin and knew exactly what could be done with one. Adroitly administered, a hatpin could inflict anything from an unanticipated discouragement to a frankly murderous and fatal attack. He also believed that Edna was capable of either. A deep stab into the ear or the eye could kill quickly. But that didn't seem likely: Smeddle didn't look as if he had been attacked, although the scratch on his face looked new. But no, if that had been Edna, she would have come and let her husband know all about it.

He spoke to Thorpe again. "Did the copper say

whether it was a man or a woman that was hurt, by any chance?"

"Not to me, no. I just heard him say that someone had been beaten up. He refused to give any more information. That was police business, he said."

"Hmm."

Gregory thought hard. Could Smeddle have hurt Edna? No, he had too much to gain from the planned theft and would never have been foolish enough to take such a risk. Anyway, Edna knew how to take care of herself.

Even so, Gregory would need to know more about the victim: were they a male or a female? If the latter, what did she look like? Edna was very attractive and any man, having seen her, would be able to describe her appearance. He simply had to know more. He would need to ascertain that Edna was definitely not still on the train, so he walked along the whole length of it and quietly checked every compartment. Most passengers would be asleep, so he would hardly be disturbing anyone. People in the sleeping berths would not have locked their compartments if they had others with them; you never knew when someone might have to visit the toilet in the middle of the night.

His walk took him the next twenty minutes and his fear strengthened when there was no sign of his wife at all. It was possible that she had taken a single sleeping-car compartment and locked herself in, but he did not think so. That would have made it difficult for her to come quickly to his support had this been necessary, and invalidated the whole reason for her being on the train. If she had committed a murder, however unlikely, she would certainly have tried to avoid the police and would have made a run for it at Crewe. This was a serious setback for him. She had been competent and decorative, and he had been lucky to find her.

Pushing these thoughts aside, Gregory noticed the station name-board as the train passed through Prestatyn. Time to collect Smeddle and prepare for the jewellery exchange.

***

Back at Crewe's main police station, the murder of Edna Clayton on the train and the maiming of Gordon Lowe on the station platform had stirred up a hornet's nest of activity. The police had examined Edna's suitcase and personal belongings as well as what they found in Lowe's pockets, and had contacted the Metropolitan Police for further information. They also contacted the police in Chester and Holyhead, requesting they keep an eye open for anything suspicious on the mail train. However, their only success was the arrest of Jeff Waterman at Chester, following a detailed description from a very angry Thumper.

Waterman had also been foolish enough to keep the letter from Lord Edale, who had incautiously signed it, and it delighted the lowly detective constable in Chester police station who read it first. "Look at this, Billy; evidence of a crime signed by a bloody lord! I bet that DCI in London will be over the moon when 'e sees this! Just make sure you get a butcher's at the London papers when we get 'em termorrer. Should give us a good laff!"

***

DCI Brown had been on duty in London and was informed of the murder, and of Thumper's attack on Lowe, and his arrest. He sat back in his chair, frowning. Although a quiet and unassuming man, he had a prodigious memory and knew how to exploit it. In half an hour he recalled what had lurked at the back of him mind when the two names came to his attention. Lowe had been a possible suspect in the rape of Lord Edale's daughter. And Clayton… well, he definitely knew him. The man who preferred to be known as Gregory. He had wanted to know about Smeddle, the jeweller about whom the police had long held suspicions.

The Crewe inspector had also informed the Met that they had arrested Thumper Dawson, who had told them about Waterman leaving him in the lurch.

"Can we nick even more birds with one stone?" muttered Brown to himself as he rang the police at Holyhead.

The duty sergeant answered the phone and Brown introduced himself, explaining, "There are two men on the Irish Mail arriving in Holyhead very soon.

And we want them interviewed as soon as possible, in relation to a murder on the train but I also have a suspicion they're up to something more. Could you hold them until I can get up there tomorrow, please?"

"The Irish Mail train sir? Yessir, I'll get some men to the harbour to pick up the two men. Could you give us some description, sir?"

Brown gave the sergeant names and details of the men and the sergeant agreed and sent five duty constables to the harbour station to hold the other two men for questioning. This was easy enough, but he decided he had better call his Chief Super as well, to let him know that the Met had requested help. Getting the Chief Super out of his bed in the middle of the night was fraught with unpleasant consequences yet not getting him out of bed could be even worse.

* * *

Passing Rhyl, Patrick handed the engine's controls over to Johnny with a grin.

"She's all yours now, Johnny. I'll take over again for the last run from Conway to Holyhead. Just watch out, and be prepared to slow down through Llandudno Junction. There could be a movement across the main lines there if these Welsh eejits allow a freight across the path of the most important train they get!"

Johnny smiled. He didn't believe that the Welsh were any different idiots than the English or the Irish, but he knew that Patrick viewed English absentee landlords in Ireland with hatred. He vividly recalled an incident some years back in the cab, when Patrick had played a joke on an arrogant English absentee landlord. He had been called to account by Authority for his behaviour, but Johnny's support at the time had saved him from serious penalty. That particular landlord had later been reported murdered on his own Irish property.

Johnny remembered too from his schooldays when his history teacher had detailed the Irish potato famine and its effects on agriculture there. Perhaps Patrick had good reason to dislike the British government of Ireland.

He eased up the regulator and they raced along the coast of North Wales, with its little holiday resorts of Abergele, Llandulas and Colwyn Bay. Johnny remembered to ease their speed at the approach to Llandudno Junction and viewed the signals ahead with relief, noting that all was clear through the busy station and junction, where the main line to Llandudno branched off.

***

In his compartment, Canon Jones woke up as the train clattered across the points at the junction. He would normally be leaving the train here because his home was at Deganwy, just a mile or so north from the junction, but on this occasion his important consultation was in Holyhead with his bishop who was on holiday there but who had asked him to visit. He was not looking forward to the meeting. The bishop was taking too great an interest in Canon Jones' private affairs.

The canon knew his private inclinations seemed to defy God's wish, according to carefully selected extracts in the Bible, but the canon was not entirely convinced by those extracts. The Church itself preached that God was Love, yet certain forms of love, it seemed, did not meet with the Church's approval. Canon Jones, though he knew the difference between love and lust, was uncertain that the Church did. His own feelings for the Llandudno priest certainly had aspects of lust, he freely admitted to himself, but didn't all love? He had personally had to remonstrate with youngsters clutching each other in an unseemly manner in church from time to time. He had even once had to speak sharply to a married couple who were obviously about to engage in a similarly intimate activity in a dark corner behind the altar at evensong. He had spoken to the minister at the time about making his sermons shorter and less boring.

While pondering on these matters, he wondered idly why two men were hurrying past in the corridor at this late hour of the morning. What was the hurry? There was at least three quarters of an hour before they reached Holyhead.

***

Gregory had walked back to find Smeddle. On this trip, he was no longer in disguise; he believed that his previous two trips in disguise would prevent anyone from regarding him as a regular traveller. Now he was familiar with the details of the run, and was consequently able to pick a suitable time for a felony. He arrived at Smeddle's compartment and entered.

"Time to make the exchange, Smeddle," he said shortly.

Smeddle got up from his seat and grabbed his small case. "Certainly, Mr Gregory. I have the exchange items ready here."

The two men walked back along the train to the luggage van, where Thorpe saw them and unlocked the door. Gregory spoke to the ex-sergeant: "The guard busy, is he?"

Thorpe replied, "Yes, Mr Gregory, he's having a break and will be occupied for at least ten more minutes." He stood up and went to a suitcase with a strong strap round it and a padlock. He undid the strap, took out a key from his pocket, and smiled at Gregory and Smeddle.

"I got the key from Sir Alexander himself." He opened the case, took out a bag, and spilled the gleaming jewels on to a small writing desk.

"Time for your expertise, Smeddle," said Gregory and Smeddle looked briefly at the roof light; it wasn't very bright, but he quickly selected half a dozen jewels, nodded at Gregory, placed them into his own bag, and replaced them with others which he had laid out ready. The whole transaction had taken two minutes and was watched carefully by Thorpe, who replaced the bag in the case and locked it. He put it carefully back exactly where it had been and locked the case again. "Well-planned, if I may say so, Mr Gregory. A very smooth operation."

"Hmm," replied Gregory. He was pleased; the whole business had gone remarkably well. The only problem now was to find what had happened to Edna, but that could wait. He had his jewels.

"Best I think if I take that bag and we separate on returning to our seats, Smeddle. We don't want to be seen together if possible. Fortunately, most passengers are well asleep. But I would like you to rejoin me in ten minutes to check over these items."

Smeddle agreed and left quickly. He was glad his part in the theft had been completed successfully. A quick check of the jewels would not take more than two minutes, then he would make his way home on a separate train from Gregory with an easy conscience and wait for his reward. There might even be, he mused hopefully, assistance he could offer Gregory in the future if the man was satisfied with his co-operation. He had been lately rather nervous about the plan, although he wasn't sure why, and the unfortunate incident on the train with that flighty bitch who had rejected his advances and then paid dearly for her rejection had upset him.

He hurried back to his seat and waited for the agreed ten minutes before he made his way back to Gregory's seat.

***

Patrick in the cab slowed the train down as they passed through Bangor on the Menai Strait and began the slow curve round to the right to tackle the Britannia tubular bridge over the water.

"You need to keep the fire door shut here, Johnny me boy," he remarked, "the roof of the bridge is close, and we don't want a blow-back."

As soon as he said it, he regretted his words; he realised that Johnny was aware of the danger, and had already prepared for it. A blow-back could cause a sudden alteration of pressure at the chimney, which could result from entering a stretch of track with a low roof overhead such as in a tunnel or, as in this case, a bridge with a low roof. It could blow the fire back into the cab, which could burn or even kill enginemen if the fire door was open. A competent fireman knowing the route would have fired sufficiently to keep the fire going through over the bridge without the fire doors open, just as Johnny clearly had.

They hastened across the bridge and swung into the sharp left-hand curve, picking up speed again as they passed the next station. Johnny looked out here with a grin. He always enjoyed trying to read the station's name, especially in the dark. It was spelled out with its 58 huge letters along the station platform from one end to the other and was a talking point throughout the principality. Locals referred to it as 'Llanfair PG' for short. However, Johnny never got further than the

'Llanfair' because on the down line the name began at the far end, and since he was usually passing it on expresses he didn't get much more on the up line either. He gave up again and turned back to his firing. This had been a much longer run than either he or Patrick had anticipated, and he was looking forward to a day's rest in Holyhead.

Patrick was also looking forward to meeting the representative from the Irish Great Southern and Western Railway. He was sure his wife and family would take the change of country in their stride, and he needed that job if he was going to be able to help his sister and look after their elderly parents.

CHAPTER 9

Anger through Anglesey

Gregory went slowly back to his seat as the train wended its way through Anglesey. The bag containing his new jewels weighed pleasantly in his pocket as he waited for Smeddle to join him once more. Their original plan had been for them to part quickly once the exchange had been made. This would ensure that nobody would be likely to realise they were associated, in case authoritative eyebrows were raised. However, the exchange had passed so smoothly that Gregory had suggested a further meeting in the train that could conceivably encourage thoughts on a further possible co-operation. He had more recently seen a rather nice item in the room of another of his wealthy associates. He was considering whether Smeddle and that new fellow Thorpe might be in a position to assist him in its acquisition.

He took the jewels out of the bag and gazed at what he believed to be the beginning of a valuable collection. They looked splendid, although not quite as they had in Sir Alexander's room; perhaps the candlelight there had been reflected rather better. Here in the night train, it was too gloomy to allow the full lustre of the colours to show their best, and in any case, they had been in a hurry to conclude their business.

Moments later, the door slid open.

"Ah, there you are, Smeddle."

Gregory pointed to the jewels laid out neatly on the seat beside him. He was clearly in an unusually good mood. "Time for you to bask in the quality of my latest jewellery collection."

Smeddle was surprised; he had never seen the man smile before. "I'd be delighted to, Mr Gregory."

He felt in his pocket for the necklace he had torn off the tart he had throttled. He hadn't examined it in the toilet at all, he had been in too much of a hurry to get away from the scene of his brutality. Back in his seat in the compartment, he had been very surprised to find that her necklace was not brass, nor were the jewels paste. They were a trio of genuine and well-cut diamonds. It was nothing exceedingly valuable, but it was certainly worth a bob or two. He had originally intended to exchange the necklace for one of Sir A's items, then changed his mind: it was too nice to simply abandon. He was not going to make a killing with it if he used it as a substitute, he knew that. Now he was thinking that he would offer it to Gregory, at a modest profit to himself, naturally.

He sat down next to the collection and was pleased

that the light in this compartment was brighter, making a detailed examination easier. He took out his pocket eyeglass, fixed it into his eye socket and peered closely at the first item, a ring onto which a ruby pendant had been mounted. He frowned, laid it quickly down, and picked up a pair of earrings. He stared at them in confusion, and then grabbed a large emerald tiepin. He glanced at Gregory, who was sitting with a smug expression on his face.

Smeddle seized another item at random and held it up for detailed examination. He stared at it in horror. These items were all fakes!

He picked others up and rapidly scanned each of them. How could he not have seen that when he checked them over in the luggage van? But the light had been very poor in there and they had been in a hurry to make the exchange. Even so, he really had been rather remiss. Mind you, they were good fakes, he would concede that. Perhaps that was the reason why he had not at first noticed their deceptive quality.

"They're all fakes, Mr Gregory!" he snapped angrily. "They're made of cheap paste!"

"What? But you checked them in the van, did you not?"

Gregory's expression was grim; this was not looking good, thought Smeddle.

"I did, sir, yes, certainly. But you must admit that the light was not good in the van, and we were in something of a hurry. Jewellery needs to be examined in clear light; daylight, for preference."

Gregory was shocked and sat thinking. His first thought was that Smeddle had somehow cheated him, but he didn't see how the man could have done that. Even if he had, he would not have been as surprised as he certainly was now. Gregory himself had been there when they saw Thorpe open the suitcase and remove the bag of jewels.

No, it couldn't possibly have been Smeddle. Was it Thorpe? Had he somehow exchanged the jewels during an earlier part of the journey? There would have been time, and he had the key of course. But what would an ex-police sergeant have known about valuable jewellery? He would have had to have replacement items made but he hadn't seen the originals in Sir Alexander's room anyway. Then again, neither had Smeddle. Thorpe didn't seem the sort who would be prepared to tackle Gregory, who had explained to him in graphic detail what happened to people who cheated on him. Who in the name of all that's holy had cheated him?

He had been staring blank-eyed at Smeddle during these cogitations and the latter became increasing nervous. He knew he had not swindled Gregory, but did Gregory know that? He wasn't sure. He did know that if Gregory had the least suspicion of him, Smeddle's future would be very short and unpleasant. Perhaps a gift of the fancy necklace would help smooth things over? That was a distinct possibility and he would not have lost anything he didn't own. The necklace, one could argue, was more in the line of a fortunate discovery – well, fortunate for Gregory at any rate. In the event, however, the word 'fortunate' could hardly be interpreted as appropriate for the occasion.

So far, Gregory was not showing any hostility; he was obviously wondering how the theft had gone so badly wrong, and Smeddle felt that this was a good time to leave the man to his meditations. He took the necklace out of his pocket. At least this was genuine, and might leave Gregory better disposed to Smeddle.

"Er, I recently picked up another little item that I thought you might like to add to your collection, Mr Gregory. I know it does not in the slightest compensate for your loss of the collection, but it is quite genuine, and the diamonds are rather nice." He took out the necklace and gave it to Gregory, who took it absent-mindedly with thanks and slid it into his pocket.

"Very good of you, Smeddle."

"Not at all, Mr Gregory. Again, I sincerely regret this unfortunate incident." He had nearly said 'error' but had changed his words just in time.

Smeddle left for his own seat again, thankful to be out of a situation which could have been rather tricky. He would take care to avoid Gregory for the next few months, to let the trouble die down. In the meantime, Gregory might have found the culprit responsible for the mishap and have taken commensurate vengeance, leaving Smeddle with a clean slate.

***

Johnny Winslowe was surprised at the amount of coal he'd had to shift over the last hour or so, after they had picked up a load in Chester's GWR shed. He had thought at the time that there would have been plenty left for the last stretch of the run to Holyhead, but this Claughton had been heavy on its use. Why was that? The run along the coast from Chester was not unduly difficult; there were no major climbs or tricky stretches. They'd had no signal checks or other annoyances common to enginemen in a hurry. So why did the engine need so much coal? At least there was enough left to take them to the harbour, no danger of running out, but even so, the locomotive had been a coal-miner's friend. He had been firing long enough to know how to use the minimum necessary for the job in hand and so save himself from having to lose a portion of his pay for over-generous use of coal. Enginemen who used more coal than was needed could expect to forfeit some of their pay, so it made sense to learn how to extract the most value out of every shovelful.

"You're having to shovel a lot, Johnny!" Patrick was also surprised; his fireman was having to work harder than he would have expected. This stretch along the coast wasn't a problem and Johnny hadn't been obviously struggling – in fact, he had never seen Johnny seriously struggling at any time in the past years they had been working together.

"I have to keep the steam up, Mr O'Leary, this engine is greedy for coal. The amount we got in Chester was only just enough."

"Aye, I can see that. We'll let 'em know that in Camden, although they've probably heard it already from other crews." Like Johnny, he was puzzled at the problem. "Half a minute." He went to the tender footplate and picked up a lump of coal. He stared at it and then looked at Johnny. "Here's the answer, Johnny," he laughed. "Those Great Western buggers in Chester have used us to get rid of some of their lower quality coal! This is freight engines' coal!"

Johnny nodded in relief: it hadn't been his poor firing. "Perhaps Crewe didn't tell them we were the Irish Mail?"

Patrick smiled, "Of course they did! They would have mentioned we were running late and were short. I wonder if some North-Western men have annoyed them recently?"

"So it might not be the Claughton's heavy coal demand?"

"Not unless the other crews have had a long stint on a Claughton and have had the same trouble. On the shorter runs it might not be so obvious but," Patrick added, "I suppose that they're new engines and any new locomotive needs thoroughly checking for minor faults the designers would want to know about and correct."

Neither Patrick nor Johnny were to know it, but the Claughtons never did get the normal full check for new locomotives. The Great War intervened, and it was another ten years before they received serious attention; when they did, it was from engineers from the rival Midland Railway, who seemed to be biased against North-Western engines.

"Ye could be right about that too," continued Patrick. "Most heavy express engines take the Euston to Crewe or the Crewe to Carlisle runs. We've just done nearly twice that, so we have. We might be the first crew to take a Claughton on such a long run."

"I wonder what it will be like to take her back out of Holyhead on an up express," Johnny said. "We've had one or two difficulties getting a heavy train up the grade out of the harbour more than once, I recall."

Patrick grinned. "I wasn't going to tell ye, Johnny, but when I was a young fireman I once got stuck on that particular grade. Me driver gave me a rough time all the way to Bangor, and the shite told everyone in the shed at Crewe North, where we were based at the time. It was years before I heard the last of it. Lucky nobody at Camden knows, so keep your gob shut, until after I've gone to Ireland!"

"You know I will, Mr O'Leary."

"Of course I know it, Johnny. What we have to do tomorrow is to make sure they fill her up with the best coal for the return run."

***

Gregory had been ruminating in his seat and wondering whether Thorpe or even Smeddle could possibly have cheated him and if so, how one of them had managed it. Firstly, neither of them seemed to have had the necessary nous to plan such a thing, and then he couldn't for the life of him see how either of them would have managed it anyway. Thorpe hadn't struck him as particularly smart, and Smeddle was certainly too timid to try anything like this on him. So what the hell had happened?

He got up and walked back to the luggage van to question Thorpe again. Thorpe looked up from his paper as Gregory tapped on the window to be let in.

"Problem, Mr Gregory?" he queried. "I didn't expect to see you again on this trip. Didn't you tell me that we should avoid being seen together after the exchange? I was sure you told me to stay away from you until you called on me in London."

"I did," Gregory spoke sharply, "but an issue has arisen."

"What issue, sir?"

"The jewels you took from the suitcase are fake."

"Fake? How could they be fake? I took them straight out of the case. You saw me." Thorpe was indignant. "Your Mr Smeddle is a jeweller, you told me. If they were fake, surely he would have noticed."

"The light in this van is not conducive to close examination, Thorpe. We only examined the jewels properly in my compartment, and they were in my pocket from here to there. Smeddle couldn't have exchanged them for fakes."

Thorpe hesitated; what he was going to say might imply an accusation against Gregory and, like Smeddle, he did not think this would be a wise move.

Gregory noticed his hesitation. "What are you about to say, Thorpe?"

His expression was cold, and Thorpe thought quickly.

"I was thinking, sir, that the fake jewels might have been put into the case with the genuine ones elsewhere in the luggage."

Gregory quickly revised his thinking: Thorpe was clearly not stupid. He could be right. "Get that key again, and we'll go through the whole case. If they're in that trunk, we haven't time to break into it. We'll be in Holyhead in half an hour."

Thorpe took the key and they opened the case again. This time, Thorpe stayed back and allowed Gregory to rifle through Sir Alexander's belongings. Furious, he found nothing. "They must be in the trunk." He stared at Thorpe and had an idea. "You were a police sergeant. Who would you pick if you wanted a reliable burglar?" he asked. "You must have come across several in your time in the force."

"Most of the good burglars I had dealings with are inside, Mr Gregory, but give me a day or two, and I'm sure I can come up with a name for you. There's a couple we knew about but weren't able to nick. I can get their addresses or contacts for you."

Gregory nodded his head. "I'll get in touch with you in London then, in a week or so." He left with the idea of getting a good burglar into Ireland once that smart bugger Alexander had settled in his new home. No damn aristocrat was going to defeat Jonathon Gregory!

***

Canon Jones didn't try to get any more sleep that night. He stared out of the window and recognised from some of the names of the little stations they passed that they were nearing Holyhead. As he did so he saw a shadow walk past in the corridor and he looked up. It was that restless character again, this time on his own. What made him walk up and down the train all night? Well, it wasn't his business anyway, the canon thought, and looked back out of the window again to ask himself when he would be able to meet up with the young priest.

The question was not a simple one. The bishop already had suspicions and Canon Gwyn Jones did not wish to increase these by any overt friendship with the young man, but he mused again over the idea beginning to take shape in his mind regarding a walking holiday. The canon patted his stomach; there was no doubt that its circumference was increasing and ought to be diminished. Walking, he had been told, was good for fitness. Might they perhaps arrange a walking holiday? Would the priest be willing? *We could leave separately and then meet at a distant hotel in the Lake District and – ?* Here his fantasies began to take over, which quickly took his mind off train-walkers with insomnia. It wouldn't be unduly difficult to request to go on leave at the same time; this would not be noticed, since they each worked in a different diocese. They could then travel separately and meet at some obscure hotel in the Lake District. After that they might – suddenly a whole new and fantastic idea occurred to him: what if they elected to go on that walk people mentioned that took them together across the Pennines to the East Coast? They would take a tent...

There was no point now in trying to catch up on any sleep: they would be arriving in Holyhead before he could doze off again. Idly, the Canon wondered again at what worries that restless character had, who spent the journey relentlessly wandering to and fro.

***

On his way to talk to Smeddle and discuss Thorpe's suggestion, Gregory put his hand in his pocket, felt the necklace again, and took it out to have a good look at what he was told was the genuine article. It seemed oddly familiar. He stepped into a toilet, shut the door and examined it again closely in a far brighter light. His eyes widened sharply. Wasn't this the necklace that he had given his wife as a Christmas present? His earlier suspicion about Smeddle's inclinations about pretty young things returned. Was he involved in Edna's disappearance? He had certainly been in the same compartment as her, and was very likely to be unaware of Edna's identity. Gregory's anger at missing the expected jewels began to metamorphose into rage at the apparent loss of his wife, and fear that in fact something far worse had happened to her than he had imagined. If Smeddle had anything to do with it, he was not going to reach Holyhead alive. The man had some questions to answer and he was going to answer them now!

Gregory stood up and returned quickly to his compartment, where he removed his jacket and tie, opened his suitcase once more and lifted the extra shirts he had packed. Underneath them was a knife in its special sheath he had bought in North Africa. The Arab who had sold it to him had also spent some time showing him how best to employ it quickly and cleanly. Gregory fastened the sheath round his waist and put his jacket back on, ensuring that the knife was invisible yet easy to pull out. He practised once or twice before he left his compartment, then strode in determined fashion along the corridor. Time to question Smeddle in every detail. This time there was not going to be any dithering or obfuscation of any sort. Smeddle was going to answer questions or face the consequences. The choice would be simple and quick; Gregory had no time for shilly-shallying.

CHAPTER 10

Horror at Holyhead

The compartment door slid open with a bang, thus wakening Smeddle, who had drifted off into a short slumber after the uncomfortable discussion with Gregory. He had tried to think of ways in which the planned theft could have been anticipated and thwarted but had failed to come up with any useful ideas.

Hopefully he'd been successful in his attempt to shore up his own innocence in the affair by the gift of the necklace stolen from that tart. Yet there was no reason he could think of that Gregory could accuse him of any part in the failure. He had been just as shocked when the collection had been seen to be a fake set of jewels. Admittedly, he had not seen the originals, but had been able to guess from the description what they had probably looked like, and had been sure that the replacements would pass casual scrutiny.

Smeddle was certain that Thorpe, an ex-copper,

would not have risked anything against Gregory, if he knew what was good for him. Gregory was not a man who believed in offering mercy to anyone. And ex-coppers sent to prison would expect to have a thin time when other prison inmates found out what they had been before. Some might even have been doing time courtesy of the ex-policemen who had arrested them, and would be eager to even the balance, as it were. Prison warders too might look the other way when vengeance was being extracted.

So why the hell had Gregory just entered with a face as black as thunder?

Smeddle felt a momentary anxiety.

"Have you found out what happened, Mr Gregory? Did Thorpe perhaps explain what might have gone wrong? I have been putting my mind to what Sir Alexander might have—"

"No!" snapped Gregory. He turned, carefully slid the door to the corridor shut, and sat opposite Smeddle. He dug into his pocket and pulled out Edna's necklace. "Tell me, Smeddle, where did you get this?"

Smeddle's blood ran cold when he saw what was in Gregory's hand. "I'm a jeweller, Mr Gregory, I get jewellery from many different sources. I do not always recall where each item came from."

"That's as maybe, Smeddle, but you must know where this necklace came from. You told me yourself: it's quite a good one. You had, you claimed, acquired it quite recently."

"That one? Let me think now. Oh yes, I believe it

came from a Frederick Harwood. Harwood is a fellow jeweller, but he also works as a fence and so gets valuable items from time to time. He offered me this necklace at a reasonable price to get rid of it quickly."

"Do you recall what his price was?"

Smeddle invented a price which he imagined Harwood would have asked. "I think he wanted thirty-five pounds for it."

"Is that what you paid him?"

"I believe so."

"Harwood," said Gregory, momentarily thinking that this was a man he could consult later when he wanted more jewellery; after he had dealt with this swine sitting in front of him.

"Now tell me, Gregory, why you are lying to me. Surely you must know that this is not a healthy thing to do."

"I'm not lying to you, Mr Gregory. You know I wouldn't do that!"

"Wrong, Smeddle. I know that you are lying to me. It surprises me that you have the nerve to do it when you know the possible consequences."

"Consequences?"

"You would regard them as serious."

"Serious?"

"Do stop repeating my words, Smeddle. I know about your liking for women, married or otherwise. You got the necklace from a woman." He held up the necklace. "Did the lady from whom you acquired this betray her lawful husband?" The thought crossed Gregory's mind that Edna might have, but he knew this was highly unlikely, not with such a poor specimen like Smeddle. She preferred young and handsome men.

Smeddle changed tactics. "I am a poor sinner, but God has given me the duty of persuading such women into the path of righteousness."

"And did He give you the right to persuade poor Mrs Clayton into the toilet on the train this evening?"

"Mrs Clayton?"

"Yes, the lady in the same compartment as yourself. The lady from whom you received this necklace."

"Was that Mrs Clayton?"

"Yes, the lady you killed." Gregory's words showed no emotion. He changed the subject. "And, purely as a matter of interest, Smeddle. Do you know my real name?"

"Is it not... Gregory?"

"No, that is my alias. My real name is Clayton. Edna Clayton, the lady you killed, was my wife."

"Oh my God!" Smeddle cried in desperation. "She tried to seduce me, Gregory, God sent me to punish her!"

"I have already made it clear to you, Smeddle, that you must not keep telling lies. God did not send you: He sent me to do what punishing is needful!"

Gregory stood up, opened his jacket and took out the long, shining knife. Smeddle's eyes stared at it in fascinated horror at what he realised was to come.

"You are about to meet your maker, Smeddle. You can explain all your various sins to Him!"

Gregory struck exactly as that North African had shown him all those months ago.

***

Canon Jones was becoming worried. His meeting with the Bishop was approaching. He tried to send his mind back to any incident which might be somehow misconstrued, but without success. Even as a youngster in his early twenties he had been aware of his feelings for other men and had tried to persuade himself that these were against God's law and thus sinful. He had failed. He had always liked ladies but had never harboured the same level of emotion that men sometimes aroused in him.

The canon was a genuinely honest man and had searched diligently through the Bible and other learned writings for answers but had never found anything which convinced him that he was evil. He was well aware that his homosexuality was generally regarded by the laws of the land as an aberration to be either cured or condemned, and was consequently careful not to behave in a manner which could give offence. His feelings were strictly illegal and if expressed and turned into action, he could be tried and found guilty. He would instantly be disowned by the Church. That was something he dreaded more than anything; he saw his work in the Church as giving meaning to his whole life. If, as seemed likely, he was going to have to forego his sexual intentions or lose his faith in God, then the young priest, and any other similar targets, would have to be sacrificed. There was no doubt whatsoever in his mind about that.

His musings were interrupted once again by the sight of a man striding grim-faced back along the corridor past his door. What was this? He seemed to have blood over his jacket! He must be badly injured, Canon Jones thought, and immediately got up to give whatever assistance he could. He followed Gregory to his compartment, where he found him sitting down, apparently unhurt.

"You seem to be covered in blood, sir. May I be of assistance at all? Are you injured somehow?"

Gregory looked up. "What? Oh, this," apparently seeing the blood on his own jacket for the first time. "Oh no, I cut myself quite badly having a last-minute shave. But look, it's very kind of you to offer, but I assure you I am quite alright."

"So there's nothing I can assist you with?"

"No, but I am grateful for your kind offer of assistance. Thank you again, Father."

As soon as the canon had left, Gregory took off his jacket. He couldn't possibly walk around with it, covered in blood as it was. He opened his window and threw the jacket out into the darkness. He took another jacket out of his case and put it on. It covered most of the blood on his shirt, although a few spots were still visible. Damn! He took another shirt out of his case and the bloodied shirt followed the jacket out of the window. Buttoning up his jacket, Gregory felt that he no longer attracted any undue attention.

That priest or whatever he was now had no evidence, were he to call the police. It was merely a question now of leaving the train for the station restaurant in Holyhead, boarding the next one back again to Euston, and planning his next attempt to relieve Sir Alexander of his jewels in Ireland. This needed careful planning; the man had shown himself to be alert, but Gregory was not a man to give up at the first failure.

He might have thought about spending more time in a different direction, had he known where the Canon was going.

***

At the rear of the train, Guard Adams walked into the luggage van.

"All well, Ted?"

"Fine thanks, Henry."

As they were talking, Canon Jones appeared and tapped on the window.

"Pardon the interruption, gentlemen," he said as they let him in, "but I believe there may be an injured man on board."

He waved vaguely towards the front of the train. "I saw him with a jacket covered in blood, and I asked if I could be of assistance to him, but he claimed to be fine. He had cut himself shaving, he said, but his chin didn't look like it had recently been shaved at all. He is in a first-class coach two coaches forward."

Guard Adams looked at Thorpe. "You stay here, Ted, and I'll go with this clerical gentleman and have a look." He turned to Canon Jones, "Please come with me, sir. You know what the man looks like."

"Of course, but I doubt whether you'll need me. He'll be fairly obvious, I would assume."

"I'd like you with me, sir, just to be sure we have the right man."

"Oh yes, of course!"

The two of them moved off along the corridor. When they came to the right coach, the canon said, "This is it; he'll be in the third compartment."

They arrived and looked in. Gregory looked up to see them and stood up quickly. Removing his knife from his jacket, he lurched towards the door. Instantly, Guard Adams put his hand firmly against the door to prevent it from sliding open. Canon Jones looked on, horrified, and added his own left hand to try and help hold the sliding door shut. With his right hand, he fumbled inside his coat to pull out an old letter.

"I'll fold this and try and push it into the gap to jam the door shut," he explained to the guard, who nodded grimly. "It might help."

The door, under Gregory's determined effort, slid open an inch or two and then came to a stop as the envelope jammed in the gap. Swearing foully, Gregory could not force the door open. He swung round, went to the outer door of the compartment and opened it, but the train was moving far too fast to risk jumping out.

"Can you hold the fort here, sir, while I go and fetch the policeman?" Henry Adams asked the canon. "The door can't open, and I won't be more than a minute or two. He's in my van."

"Quickly then," replied the canon and the guard hurried off. Canon Jones put his foot behind the edge of the sliding door to prevent it from being forced back, as Gregory came back to try the door again. Two minutes later, the guard returned with Edward Thorpe.

As soon as Gregory saw Thorpe, he smiled and relaxed, putting his knife away again into his jacket. He was now safe from the stupid churchman and that ignorant guard. They had no idea that Thorpe was one of his men.

Edward Thorpe pulled out the jammed paper, opened the door and entered the compartment with Henry and the canon behind him.

"Nice to see you again, Mr Gregory," he said. "You really don't need that knife, sir."

Gregory nodded. "Thank you, Thorpe. Good to see that you have proved rather more useful than I had originally anticipated."

"Yessir," replied the sergeant and then, walking further into the compartment, he briskly seized Gregory by the shoulders, twisted him round, and snapped a pair of handcuffs on him, removing the knife from Gregory's jacket.

"What the hell?" raged Gregory. "What on earth are you doing, man?"

"Jonathon Clayton, also known as Jonathon Gregory,

I'm arresting you for a possible murder, attempting a theft, threatening a train guard and passengers with a knife, and for resisting arrest by a policeman."

"But you're not a policeman; you were sacked from the force!"

Sergeant Thorpe smiled as he heard that. "DCI Brown will be very pleased to know that his suspicions were confirmed, sir."

"But I heard him call for your dismissal!"

"Indeed, you did. You were supposed to hear that call for me to be disciplined but it wasn't real. The Chief Inspector suspected you of planning a theft and I was to discover whether you were, and to keep him informed."

As they took Gregory back to the luggage van, and fastened him tightly to a stanchion, Thorpe remarked, "There was another man with him. I think he was a jeweller. I know who he is. We must go and find him on the train."

"Sir,' he addressed the canon, "will you accompany us again? The jeweller is not a violent man; he's too fat anyway."

The canon agreed and they set off down the train. Thorpe was leading the way, when he suddenly stopped as they reached the compartment where Smeddle was.

"Oh my God!" he gasped and put his hand out to stop the canon from coming closer.

"What is it?" asked the canon, bumping into him. The sergeant held up his hand to stop the canon from going closer.

"You really don't need to see this, sir. There's a dead man on the seat. It's the jeweller. He has been stabbed, and there's blood everywhere." He went in himself and checked Smeddle's pulse. Looking back at the other two, he shook his head. "Dead as a doornail."

Canon Jones was horrified. Henry Adams looked into the compartment and was shocked at what he saw but immediately considered the practical consequences. He walked past Sergeant Thorpe into the compartment before the policeman could stop him.

"Don't touch anything, Henry!" called Thorpe. "There will be valuable evidence there!"

"No, I won't, Ted. But we can't leave the compartment open for anyone to walk in." He ushered the sergeant out again, pulled down the window shades to block any sight of the horror inside, slid the door shut and took out a key to lock it, until more police could arrive.

"They'll have to detach this coach; they can't possibly let it go back to Euston in this state," Adams muttered to himself. "It'll have to be thoroughly cleaned before they re-attach it to a train."

As he spoke, the train began to slow down for the approach to the Holyhead harbour terminus. They hurried back with Canon Jones to confront Gregory in the luggage van. He was sitting gloomily when the three men came in.

"You've knifed your partner, you utter swine!" called Adams angrily to Gregory. "The poor bugger's lying dead, covered in his own blood. What will he get, Ted?"

"Well, he won't spend much time in prison, that's for sure." Thorpe stared at Gregory. "You'll swing for that, mate; I can guarantee it!"

"The killing surprises me greatly," Thorpe added to his companions. "My guv'nor told me that Gregory here was careful. But we really didn't think he was such a fool." He addressed Gregory again. "Fancy, killing a man and keeping the knife on your person! Still, it makes the case for the prosecution much easier. At least I imagine we'll find your bloody clothing somewhere along the line not too far away. I'll warn the Welsh coppers to look for it."

Gregory simply glared at him helplessly. Canon Jones closed his eyes in pain; he knew there would soon be a hanging. He didn't approve of judicial killing under any circumstances, yet he could not feel any sympathy for the murdered Smeddle.

***

Patrick eased the train to a gentle stop at the harbour terminus and Johnny climbed down to uncouple the coaches, ready for the little tank engine to attach at the rear and draw them out to the carriage sidings. Here they would be cleaned and prepared for the return journey to Euston the following evening.

Patrick looked at his fireman. "Ye did well again, Johnny. Ye'll be drivin' yerself soon!"

"Well, if I am, it'll be thanks to you, Mr O'Leary,"

grinned Johnny. "You've always given me plenty of advice and practice, and," he added, "I hope your interview with the Great Southern and Western man goes well. Do you want me to come with you?"

"Not yet, Johnny, but I'll call ye if he wants to talk to ye." Patrick pulled out his watch. "Aye, I'd better be gettin' over to see him; I don't want to be late. I'll catch up with ye in the enginemen's mess in an hour or so."

He left and headed for the station offices. Johnny continued to clean the cab to make it ready for the duty enginemen to take it to the shed. It would be serviced thoroughly before it was ready for a return duty back to its home shed at Camden.

He went to the enginemen's mess for a mug of tea and a bite and considered what he would say if asked about the Claughton's performance. He had been impressed by the power of the big engine, but there were a couple of minor matters he would mention. The only other difficulty was the excessive use of coal. There was little doubt that the engine could manage the long run, but he couldn't see it being much use on a through run from Euston to Carlisle. It would need to be coaled again on the way, and the unfortunate fireman would have plenty of shovelling, especially if his driver wasn't prepared to take over the shovel from time to time. Seven or eight hours' shovelling so much coal would be well beyond the ability of most firemen, Johnny thought. He would have been close to exhaustion if his driver hadn't helped out twice on the long run. Still, the coal companies would be happy.

As he was pondering all this, Patrick came into the mess, sooner than Johnny had expected; he hoped this didn't mean bad news. But Driver O'Leary had a huge grin on his face.

"I've got the job, Johnny! I'll be drivin' in Ireland in two months, so I will!"

"Congratulations, Mr O'Leary! That's great news – for you at least. Not so good for me, of course. I'll miss you."

"When I've got the missus and the kids settled, I'll write to ye, and I'll want ye to come over and see us all. Right now, let's go and see where we can kip, an' what we'll be drivin' tomorrow back to Euston."

***

In his London office, Chief Inspector Brown sat with Sergeant Thorpe. Both men were smoking cigars.

"All entirely satisfactory, Ted, thanks to your able assistance," commented the DCI.

"Hardly, sir," replied Edward Thorpe, surprised at the use of his Christian name. "It was your suspicions about the unfortunate Smeddle followed by your quick remark within Gregory's hearing that set it all off. I was merely the messenger boy, with very clear instructions as to what I had to do."

"Nevertheless, you followed them intelligently. By the way," Brown added, "had you noticed that I didn't address you by your title?"

"It did cross my mind."

"There was a reason for that," the DCI was grinning broadly now, "Inspector."

Inspector? Thorpe glanced behind him, surprised that he hadn't heard an inspector come in. But there was nobody else there.

He looked again at his boss, frowning.

"Yes," the other nodded. "Between us, you and I have nailed two men who have been a major thorn in police sides for quite a long time. I've been thinking about this for some time anyway and yesterday I sent a request to the Commissioner. This morning it returned with his signature on it."

Thorpe was till puzzled. "Sir?"

"I have a new deputy: Inspector Edward Thorpe." Detective Chief Inspector Brown held out his hand. "Congratulations, Ted. As from today, you are Detective Inspector Thorpe, and my official deputy."

Epilogue

The remaining threads of this tangled tale are easily unravelled. Driver O'Leary went to Ireland to follow a rewarding career, retiring from railway service as a locomotive inspector in 1924.

Johnny Winslowe's career followed a similar path and he retired from the LMS, first in 1938 before rejoining for the duration of the war, and then again in 1945.

James Dixon married Harriet in Gretna as planned, before he joined up to serve in the Royal Flying Corps in 1915, discovering a surprising ability to pilot a plane and, even more surprisingly, he survived the war to remain in the RAF. He and Harriet had three children.

Lady Marchant returned to London but finding that gossip about her was still rife, retired to live out her remaining years quietly near Manchester. She passed away in 1931, leaving a remarkably rich gardener.

Canon Jones enjoyed his walking tour with his young friend, later served as a padre in the army, and remained very discreet, finally retiring in 1925.

Messrs Waterman and Thumper Dawson served two years each in prison before being released to serve in the army; both died courageously at Paschendaele.

Gordon Lowe recovered from his injuries and, unfit for the army, became a businessman, before being shot in 1922 by a crime boss he tried to swindle.

Lord Edale served ten years in Broadmoor before being released to discover that his estate was worthless because his daughter had used it to finance an extravagant lifestyle in the south of France.

Also by Michael Clutterbuck

Mayhem on the Margate: Rumbles on the Rails Book One

In wartime Birkenhead, tragedy strikes when a gang of mischievous children ignore their parents' warnings and play amid the bombsites. It soon becomes clear that the local hospital has been the victim of some black-market activity and the substandard medicine fails to do its job. A boy who should have been saved has lost his life.

Retired Detective Inspector Roger Wolseley has seen enough greedy chancers making capital from the war and makes it his mission in retirement to hunt down the criminal behind the knock-off drugs. He soon has his man and is hot on his tail, heading for the South Coast on the Margate Express.

A young family become unintentionally entangled in Wolseley's escapades, and fans of Michael Clutterbuck's Steaming Into books will be delighted to find Driver George Denton and Fireman Lance Hargreaves also have a role to play.

The Steaming Into Series:

a fantastic collection of tales from the rails

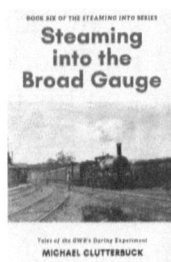

www.ingramcontent.com/pod-product-compliance
Lightning Source LLC
Chambersburg PA
CBHW030301100526
44590CB00012B/475